Principles of Modern Educational Psychology

Dr. Marwan Abuhewaij

 www.trafford.com

North America & International
toll-free: 1 888 232 4444 (USA & Canada)
phone: 250 383 6864 • fax: 812 355 4082

Table of Contents

Unit One
Educational Psychology

Unit Two
Instructional Objectives

Unit Three
Intelligence

Unit Four
Cognitive Development

Unit Five
Motivation and Attention

Introduction

The research in this book discusses the principles on which modern educational psychology stands for. Such principles have been selected to meet the aspirations of those in charge of the educational process and to update their persistent outlook towards the direction of the learner as a creative energy of no limits. Such direction requires the verification of knowledge related to the principles of education and educational psychology along with the nature and process of modern education and learning. Especially those researches in these fields still rapidly developing since the recent years, if the researches resulted in modern psychological facts concerned with the learner. As the learner is considered the center of the educational process, material and purpose, at the time the educational process explores the nature of the environment with all its elements as the environment is considered the field of education and its medium effective in both education and learning.

The subject of this book came as a fruit of effort in which good choice was more difficult than writing. This subject is a subject that resulted from the writing of many of the best scientists. Those scientists have preceded us in the research and examination of topics of Modern Educational Psychology and in the definition of affairs and concerns of rapidly developing and moving science… We have ensured that many of the concepts shall be presented as contained in the writings of their authors.

Subsequently, we tried as much we can-through the contents of this book of a total of five units-to connect between the concepts, despite their number and the diverting of views therein. We also tried to conclude results expected for all recent fields of educational psychology in order to enrich the subject of this science. Such science has entered the world of humanity from the widest doors. By enrichment, there is an increase of reviving and developing of the future.

As we provide topics of this book, we hope that the fact of the place of educational psychology in a world in which researches of this humanitarian science has been developed, be a step in the process of research and follow up. I have concluded to cognitive facts that teachers and learners must observe and be aware likewise.

Dr. Marwan Abu Hewaij
Monterey-CA
October 2010

Description of the Book:

The subject of this book discusses the modern educational psychology regarding its definition, relationship with branches of psychology, principles, aims and methods of research. Also, this subject discusses the educational aims regarding their levels along with behavioral objectives components, dimensions and formulation. The subject focuses on the basic concepts of development and its theories, processes and characteristics. The subject also studies fields of intelligence, remembering and motivation.

Aims of the Book:

The subject of this book aims to enable the researcher of the essence of educational psychology to be more effective. The subject shall acquire him the following:

1- Comprehensive view of the educational psychology, its definition, aims and principles.

2- Skill of preparing behavioral objectives.

3- Understanding the process and stages of the student's development and what resulted in appropriate dealing methods.

4- Understanding the subject and applications of humanitarian intelligence.

5- Understanding motivation, its importance in educational achievement and the methods of improving motivation in learners.

Unit One

Educational Psychology

Contents:

First: Definitions of Educational Psychology

Scientists and researchers reached more than one definition for educational psychology. Although these definitions varied in their explanations of the definition of this science, yet they are in whole place educational psychology above all in the service of educational reform. Multiplicity of endeavors that defined this science is maybe due to the comprehensive perception of the subject of educational psychology. Where this subject constitutes a mixture of scattered and combined subjects, most of which belong to other branches of psychology. In addition, this science, in each of its development stages, was subject to new tasks added to it, which increased the expansion of its field.

In this regard, we will discuss some of the definitions of educational psychology for Arab scientists and researchers, as contained in the mothers of Arabian books specialized in educational psychology.

Definitions of Arab scientists and researchers of educational psychology:

Definition of Dr. Abdul Rahman Adas:

Educational psychology is a group of studies directed to know how learning occurs and how teaching helps in its occurrence.

Definition of Dr. Jaber Abdul Hameed Jaber:

Educational Psychology has two meanings:
First: An outdated meaning that educational psychology is an application for the results of psychology in the education field.
Second: Educational psychology is a branch of psychology that studies educational problems by using psychological approaches, and by methods and concepts developed for this purpose.

Definition of Dr. Fuad Abu Hatab:

Educational psychology is the scientific study of human behavior, which resulted during the educational processes.

Dr. Fuad Abu Hatab cites a definition by (Ausubel and Robinson) that: "Educational psychology is a group of relationships derived experimentally or logically between factors (or variables) in the school attitude and desired results (as measured by the actual behavior indicators for students).

Dr. Abu Hatab defines educational psychology in term that: "Educational psychology is one of the main curriculum necessary for training teachers in the education faculties and institutions, for preparing educators and instructors in training and rehabilitation programs of different types and levels, and for preparing psychologists and social workers working in the school field. Educational psychology even may expand to all fields that prepare individuals to work in any field seeking to control and adjust the human behavior (such as medicine and mass media).

Definition of Dr. Ahmad Zaki Saleh:

Educational psychology is the science that examines the problems of educational development as practiced by the school, where school is the institution chosen by the community to oversee the education of the youth. In this research educational psychology is characterized in being an applied theoretical science.

Second: Relationship between Educational Psychology and Branches of General Psychology

The position of educational psychology becomes obvious between human sciences by studying the relationship that connects this science with human sciences. Of the most prominent among these relationships is the general psychology exemplified in its subdivided schools and approaches from which the educational psychology is considered a branch therefrom. The position also becomes by clarifying the relationship of educational psychology with other sciences.

- The relationship of educational psychology with schools and approaches of general psychology:

Philosophy was formed with time, and then by the way of natural development psychology and other sciences had separated from it. We also find that psychology itself was naturally developed and its components were formed. It is known that psychology aims utmost at understanding the human behavior that is not limited to one field but extends into many different fields.

Whereas the aim of psychology was to reveal the basics of human behavior, it is necessary-for achieving this end-to study this behavior in its different fields. Therefore, psychology has branched into different branches and its components were formed. Industrial psychology, social psychology, mental health awareness, child psychology, developmental psychology, experimental psychology, psychometrics and therapeutic psychology were emanated from educational psychology.

Educational psychology has a common limit with education, and another with psychology. In fact, the difference in point of views still exits about whether educational psychology is a part of education or a part of psychology?

Dr. Jaber Abdul Hameed indicates that this issue is raised in the Arabian arena and is provoked by not small group of psychologists working in faculties of art. The common trend among these psychologists is to take out workers in educational psychology from the group of those specialized in psychology. The position of psychology between these two specializations requires from its workers to master the basics of both fields because they will benefit from of them together. They also required from them to be proficient in two languages, psychology and education. Without being proficient in both languages, they will have a difficulty in understanding and dealing with educators from one hand and with psychologists from the other hand.

Dr. Jaber continues and decides that the educators' attitude from educational psychologists is not much different from the attitude of psychologists in the faculties of art and others. Many educationalists look at workers in educational psychology the same way they look to strange elements in education, because from their point of view they use idiomatic language not suitable for the practical and applied aspects in education. At the same time, we find that psychologists look at the language of educational psychologists as hybrid and mixed language.

Educational psychology represents one of the applied branches of psychology; however, it is not separated from other branches of this science, whether were basic or applied.

The following are explanations of these relationships between educational psychology and other branches of general psychology:

1- Experimental Psychology:

Experimental psychology concerns with studying problems related to psychological phenomena. Concerns of experimental psychology focus on animal behavior and psychological phenomena, which attracted the attention of those concerned with education problems in these psychological researches conducted in psychology laboratories, especially of what is provided by its results of solutions for problems of school learning such as programmed education and teaching devices. The biggest contribution of experimental psychology exemplified in developing the scientific and experimental trends of those concerned with education problems.

2- Social Psychology:

The teacher needs what social psychology provides of results that increase his understanding of the dynamics of group and its effects in the behavior of its members. Therefore, we find in the time being an increased trend of a number of educational psychologists towards the consideration of their field as applied social psychology as long as social psychology helps in connecting between elements of the educational attitude in a functional framework.

3- Developmental Psychology:

This science studies changes that occur in the human behavior in various stages of life. It concerns with the study of development of children and adolescents, whom are the greatest consumers of the educational process in which educational psychology concerns with ….. Also, the largest contributions provided by experts in this field came from the researches of cognitive and emotional development and social learning field. It was also helpful in identifying the early trends and the environmental circumstances that clearly influence in the development of intellectual abilities and personality traits in children, adolescents and adults.

4- Clinical Psychology:

Psychologists specialized in psychological guidance and supervision, social and psychological service and mental health often use many researches of clinical approach that depends on collecting observations on the behavior of individuals who need individual assistance because of emotional difficulties. Some of these researches were helpful in solving problems and difficulties related to emotional behavior in the educational attitudes whether were connected to the behavior of teachers or learners.

5- Psychometrics and Educational Assessment:

Psychometrics, such as intelligence measurement, mental abilities and personality trends, had made a significant contribution in specifying the field of psychology from the beginning. Then interest in educational assessments generally increased in seeking to achieve one of the important requirements of sciences, quantitative accuracy. Therefore, quantitative programs were emerged that focus on what can be measured from academic achievement, such as information memorization and skills acquisition. Scientists of psychometrics were recently able to invent approaches that can be used in testing some aspects of cognitive behavior that seemed difficult in testing (like creative thinking) in addition to testing aspects of emotional, temperamental and social behavior.

Educational psychology did not stop at the limits of verifying the validity of application of educational principles only, but it was able to create many methods concerned with the research of educational problems that did not attract the attention required from general psychology. For example, those modern types including activity and projects methods, diagnosis and treatment of learning difficulties, teaching various subjects, methods used in estimating the educational achievement, improvement of training approaches in kindergarten and scientific guidance and adult education, all of which are fields of specialists in educational psychology. These fields have not been tackled by general psychology except with limited study.

Within the framework of scientific approach of educational psychology, it is noticed that the specialist in educational psychology adopts special scientific line that differs to some extent from the point of view of educational psychologist whose efforts are directed towards searching for and achieving general principles. While the first is basically concerned with searching for and achieving practical solutions for problems, the aim of the educational psychologist is to develop valuable professional approaches, while the aim of the general psychologist is to establish a structure of general scientific principles.

On the other hand, we find that Dr. Ahmad Zaki Saleh believes that educational psychology, as being the scientific methodological study for the process of educational or teaching development, can not be considered as a branch of psychology and applied on education, yet it is one of the sections of psychology branches that specializes in studying the educational development, such as social psychology that studies the social phenomenon, and psychopathology that studies inconsistency between personality and its domain.

Dr. Ahmad Zaki concludes that educational psychology is one of the branches of psychology that deals with educational development. In this study educational psychology is characterized of being a theoretical applied science.

Relationship of Educational Psychology with Other Human Sciences

Sciences in the ancient ages were limited to the study of natural phenomena, especially physical phenomena. With passage of time, development begins to occur on the course of sciences when exceeded to the stage of studying biological phenomena, which achieved significant successes in this regard. The evidence on such is the history of life, embryology, anatomy, physiology and other fields of human sciences.

Success of this experimental approach in human sciences had largely contributed in the expansion of its activities to study the behavioral phenomena, as these sciences become directed towards the field of scientific activity exemplified in experimental methods to study the human behavior. Therefore, it was a pioneer step in strengthening bonds of relationship between different human sciences, such as general psychology from which educational psychology and all other branches of sciences were emerged, all of which are human sciences that fused in the crucible of the experimental approach, like the other sciences.

Consequently, development, which occurred in applying the experimental sciences on our daily life and on the social function of science, is a development occurred in fields of human sciences, including educational psychology as being studying the human being who constitutes the main hub for human effort and activity in all fields which emphasize that strong relationship existing between educational psychology and human sciences from one hand, and between it and other experimental sciences from other hand.

In the context of roles' similarity between educational psychology and other human sciences, Dr. Fuad Abu Hatab believes that educational psychology is playing regarding education the same role played by mathematics, physics and chemistry to medicine and engineering.

Physician who practices tasks of diagnosis and treatment needs, besides his deep knowledge in biology, cultural, social and environmental awareness, as well as the engineer who designs a system, needs thorough knowledge in psychics, mathematics and chemistry. Furthermore, he needs aesthetic, economic and political understanding.

The same applies on educators, teachers, supervisors and instructors; they must combine between the foresight formed by educational psychology, philosophical reasoning, social awareness, economic analysis and political knowledge.

Dr. Abu Hatab concludes by saying that judgments and values without knowing the facts of science are not more effective than knowing the facts of science without the availability of social sensitivity and valuable judgments.

Third: Components of Educational Psychology, its Subjects and Characteristics:

- Subjects of Educational Psychology:

Field of educational psychology expands to extend to subjects that start from adjusting behavior, managing class, studying motivation in classroom and studying social development. It also extends to cognitive psychology for school subjects. It may be a basic research or be an application in serving problems and finding solutions thereof.

Many attempts were made to specify the subjects of educational psychology. All results indicated that this science is a diverse field. In the middle of this diversity and differentiation there is a little of agreement.

One of the most prominent attempts made in search of basic subjects and concepts for educational psychology is Englander attempt in 1976, where he asked from the educational psychology teachers to arrange (75) concepts. It was found that all respondents had selected the following concepts as subjects of educational psychology:

1- Adjustment of behavior as a key concept of leading position.

2- Group of development concepts such as readiness, development theory of (Piaget) and endogenous and exogenous motives.

3- Self concept and level of ambition.

While concepts that received the higher agreement in teaching and learning are procedural conditioning and learning by discovering. In the field of testing there was relatively high agreement on the mastery-learning performance objectives.

In 1977, Feld-Hosen, one of the educational psychology learners, had called to arrange twenty subjects in terms of their importance as a basic curriculum in educational psychology. They found that the concerned subjects that are necessary for teaching are limited in four, namely: education and teaching, motivation, learning results and testing and tests.

On the other hand, we find that Arther Gates in his book, composed in 1923 in title of (Psychology for Education Students), determines four main subjects for educational psychology in cooperation with three of his colleagues who participated with him in writing this book in its new copy. The four subjects are as follows:

1- Development of the individual in its various stages, in terms of mental, physical and emotional development from birth to maturity.

2- Mental health in terms of adaptation and development of personality, methods of diagnosis and treatment of maladaptation, problems of underdeveloped students and mental health for the student and the teacher.

3- Measurements and tests, intelligence measurement, special abilities, diagnosis of special defects, and estimation and correction of progress in education.

4- Learning processes, thinking and reasoning, art and approaches of teaching and problems of organizing curricula.

Also from the other hand, we find that (Horas. B. English), of Ohio University, submits-without any attempt to organize- a list of subjects that the student interested in books of educational psychology will find. He cites a group of subjects related to the general subject of individual differences, or to problem of treatment of students each according to his nature: special abilities- defect aspects and up-normal children (geniuses or unintelligent children)-misdemeanant young-(emotionally unstable child and the child who has mobility impairment… etc). Problems of vocational and educational education and supervision and its relationship in differences: tendencies, attitudes, ideals, emotions and abilities.

There is also a group of subjects related to activity aspects that the teacher makes such as authority, regulation, mental health at classroom, finding the appropriate circumstances that help in learning and social psychology in relation of classroom.

Finally, there is a group of subjects related to the production of the school as a group of problems related to educational politics, estimation of progress, psychology of learning in their application on special subjects, dynamic and manual skills, creative activity aspects, thinking, creation, personal protection from inconsistency, and creation of happy personal life.

While Dr. Ahmad Zaki Saleh believes that the general subject of educational psychology is limited in the practical study of the process of educational development, based on the fact that educational psychology specializes in examining problems of educational development as practiced by the school-that institution selected by the community to supervise the education of the youth.

Therefore, subjects of educational psychology can be determined-as Dr. Ahmad Zaki Saleh believes-by specifying the function of school from one hand, and by what meant in the process of educational psychology from the other hand, according to the following:

First: Behavioral elements for educational aims, which is the behavioral term for general educational aims.

Second: General development cycle, which means here the total general development of the personality. Whereas studying the main traits in each of the development stages allows the curricula authors to match between these traits and the curriculum aims. In addition, studying development is connected with another subject of high importance which we call development requirements.

Third: Learning problem: Functions of school can not be achieved except by learning process. We would like to give the child the right healthy habits and some habits that help his body to grow healthy. In addition, we would like to habituate him on particular mental habits like the ability of criticism without offending, habit of substantive thinking, habit of scientific approach in discussion, habit of reading and seeing, and to habituate him on social habits such as self respect and respect others and habit of up holding his freedom and freedom of others, all of which are problems and subjects that learning psychology deals with.

Fourth: Study of intellectual abilities: On the other hand, we find that Dr. Fuad Abu Hatab believes that subjects of educational psychology exemplified by the proper psychological principles that deals with problems of education and school learning matters. Such principles must be provided to teachers and other workers in fields of adjusting the human behavior.

In this context, Dr. Abu Hatab presented the results of analyzing the content conducted in Yale in 1971 for the main writings of educational psychology amounting at that time one hundred books. He found that the most frequent subjects are the following:

1- Cognitive, psychical, emotional, creative and social development.

2- Learning processes and its theories, measurement methods and determining its affecting factors. In addition, subjects of transfer of training effect, readiness to learn, teaching methods, guidance of learning, and organization of learning attitude.

3- Intelligence measurement, intellectual abilities, personality traits and achievement, and basics of building achieved tests or conditions of psychological and educational tests.

4- Social interaction among students and between students and teachers.

5- Mental health for individual and social and school consistency.

In the context of the course of modern educational psychology, Dr. Abu Hatab believes that this science is directed towards much of determination of its subject, as it is no longer a mixture of learning theory, development psychology, mental health and psychological and educational testing. However, it had its own independent and distinguished entity, thanks to the use of modern scientists systems to systems language in it.

System means in Arabic (Nasaq "نسق", netham "نظام" or Jehaz "جهاز" all of which are used in Arabic as a translation of the word (system). It is called on a group of merged regulated relationships that links between interacting parts each pattern is resulted from that lead to a certain function. Such system may be in any of level of complexity or composition; therefore, it is called as an example on the solar system, international system, microorganism, circulatory system in the body, computer and human engineering, even on a small machine or simple system. Then at our time it is called on the educational processes.

Perception of the educational process as a system helps in determining the subject of educational psychology. In this regard, Dr. Abu Hatab believes that the most common perceptions here are the form of four components proposed by (Robert Glairs) in 1962, namely: educational aims, inlet behavior, process and approaches of learning and educational evaluation. It seems that subjects or components-according to Dr. Abu Hatab's opinion-form the best system of the field of educational psychology.

While Dr. Abdul Rahman Adas, in his modern view on educational psychology, emphasizes that it is difficult on any individual among us to practice teaching sufficiently and effectively if he did not address in one way or another to the subjects of educational psychology. He mentions brief history of each of the subjects contained in this science classified into five wide classes, as follows:

1- Awareness of the students' characteristics: (It means here explanation of the characteristics of children in differed ages of growth stages.

2- Understanding the learning process: Regarding learning includes occurring of change in behavior; as well it includes change in thoughts and thinking methods. This is for the so-called cognitive theories in learning.

3- Creation of effective atmosphere for learning, the requirements for doing so are to motivate students, i.e. finding the appropriate methods to excite the students regarding curriculum subjects and transfer their energy toward learning.

4- Taking into consideration differences among students (i.e. consideration of individual differences).

5- Using evaluation property.

Characteristics of Educational Psychology:

One of the most prominent characteristics of educational psychology is the following:

1- Independence

Many of the students still decide that educational psychology is a group of facts derived from various branches of psychology. In other words, this science provides applications for principles of general psychology on education.

However, educational psychology and efforts made to upgrade it led to significant changes in the nature of this science. The educational psychologist can not wait until basics, useful from studies that discusses other purposes, are occurred to him. But he quickly search independently in the psychological aspects for all educational problems by using any of the principles or curricula of research used in other psychological studies if he was sure that they meet his purpose. However, the educational psychologist will not hesitate in adjusting them or (devise new curricula from them whenever he deems appropriate.)

This means that educational psychology becomes standing as the accurate reviewer from every opinion that calls for the application of any of the psychological principles on educational attitude that does not mean more than following one particular method. This particularly true on many applications made by psychologists and others whose their knowledge in curricula and teaching methods was accidental.

2- Drawing Practical Educational Results from Various Psychological Theories and Principles:

This characteristic makes the educational researcher gain new type of skill and perception in interpreting facts. He in this regard tries to learn how to explain what various general theories and principles include of the results of an educational process. Also, the theoretical principles that based from those differences resulted from the difference of educational approaches. Therefore he first draws psychological facts and basics. He then concludes the practical educational application afterwards.

3- Specialization:

Specialization becomes one of the characteristics that educational psychology characterized by. Educational psychology is no longer limited in the function of verifying the validity of application of education principles only, but it creates a group of curricula of dealing with educational problems that has not received curative treatment from general psychology. For example, teaching various subjects, especially applying modern types of activity of curricula and projects, diagnosis and treatment of educational difficulties, modern methods for estimating scientific achievement, improving teaching approaches in kindergarten schools, adults education and educational guidance, all of which are examples from the nature of specialization for workers in the field of educational psychology.

4- Principle of Experiment and Scientific Research:

Educational psychology did not stop in its educational applications in the point of satisfaction of theoretical concepts. However, educational psychology went beyond the stage of building the scientific evidence on the validity of such application, using from experiment a mean to verify the application of psychology on education.

Fourth: Aims of Educational Psychology, its Emergence and Development

Aims of Educational Psychology:

Dr. Ahmad Zaki Saleh determines the aim of education psychology based on the definition we had mentioned before by saying that this is the science that looks at the problems of educational development as practiced by the school.

It is meant from educational development mentioned in this definition that educational development is all aspects in which the school is interested. Accordingly, Dr. Ahmad Zaki believes that the aim of educational psychology in light of such is determined according to two concepts:

First concept: If the purpose of school was limited to gain knowledge, collect information and study lessons, then the aim of educational psychology is to handle the methods of developing such knowledge and creates means that help the child in achievement and acquire these cognitive habits.

Second concept: If the function of the school was wider than this, i.e. aims to take care of the child as a future citizen, then the function concerns with his personality in various aspects, takes care in his general health, develops his tendencies and readiness, motivates his intellectual and professional abilities, develops social tendencies that helps him understand his relationships with others and accustoms him the creative method in filling his spare time. Therefore, studying educational psychology for educational development must include all these characters.

While Horas B., English, of the state of Ohio University, believes that educational psychology aims to look independently at psychological aspects for all practical educational problems, by using in this regard any of the principles or curricula of research used in other psychological studies, i.e. educational psychology follows the direct psychological study for educational problems.

Dr. Abdul Rahman Adas concludes from his definition of educational psychology that: "Educational psychology is a group of studies directed to know how learning occurs, and how teaching helps the occurrence of learning." He concludes that this science aims through information that included in this science to look at the teachers' characters, their developmental characteristics and how they learn certain behaviors and thoughts. This science also aims to study circumstances that can lead to learn the best they have, to conclude how the needs of students can be met in various capabilities and backgrounds and how to evaluate the resulted learning.

In order to achieve educational psychology these aims, it derives its instructions from a number of various psychological theories and directions, aiming to find answers for questions like:

-   Why and how children learn?

-   How can the teacher motivate students to make them want what they need from learning?

-   Are young children different from oldest ones in their learning?

-   How can the teacher teach class-effectively-with students that differ a lot in their capacities and backgrounds?

-   Can education be evaluated effectively-if yes, how?

All these subjects mentioned by Dr. Abdul Rahman Adas represent, by its own, the aims expected from educational psychology to achieve in the framework of the possibility of helping the teacher to teach in a better way and to enjoy the interaction between him and his students more largely-according to the opinion of Dr. Adas himself.

It is noticed from this scientific analysis of the aims of educational psychology that Dr. Abdul Adas meets with what concluded by each of Ausubel and Robenson when they defined educational psychology as a group of relationships derived experimentally or logically from factors (or variables) in the school attitude and the desired outcomes (as measured by the actual behavior indexes for students).

We also find that Dr. Fuad Abu Hatab, who mentioned this definition, meets with Dr. Abdul Rahman Adas regarding: "the fundamental task of educational psychology is to provide teachers and other workers in fields of adjusting the human behavior with the proper psychological principles that deals with education problems and matters of school learning in order that they become deeper understanding, more aware of and more flexible in various educational attitudes."

Although Dr. Abu Hatab goes much further than that, he believes that services of educational psychology are not limited to school field only. However, this science extends in its aims to include all fields that prepare individuals for working in a field that seeks to control human behavior and adjusting it (such as medicine and mass media).

Emergence of Educational Psychology:

Educational psychology has a short history; it is not long-standing as being a field of specialization of human sciences fields. The researcher through the history of science rarely finds a science emerged and developed in a short time like educational psychology although it had a long past. Although the passage of long years before this science became special, its roots in the early philosophical jurisprudences that connected with human are no space to discuss. However, it can be returned to the references specialized in this regard, where philosophical writings since ancient times showed interest in educational and psychological matters, such as knowledge of phenomenon that surrounds us in the world of people and things (learning) and tools that enable as to know (mind and senses).

Johann Frawdwick Herbert-(1776-1841) was the first missionary of educational psychology or education as an applied field of psychology. He tried before more than one hundred years to infer from psychology-which started to be separated at that time from philosophy-the principles that appeared valuable for schools at the time being, those principles that emerged under the name of educational psychology. Herbert attempt was successful; however, few except the specialized student realize how much he owes to this practical educational system to this day.

At the time that Herbert's activities were emerging, each of Herbert Spencer (1820-1903), Thomas Hecksley (1825-1895) and Charles Eliot (1834-1920) were the pioneers of scientific school for formal training. They were interested in inheritance and environment problems that directed Francis Jalton (1812-1911) to visit the field of mental measurement who advanced in far scientific strides by James Cattell (1860-1944), Alfred Binet (1857-1911) and others, which is a field that contributed prominently in determining the milestones of modern educational psychology.

Boranj allocates twelve pages in his book (History of Experimental Psychology) for the history of educational psychology. Most of the pages deal with the history of mental measurement in Jalton, Cattell, Spearman and Thruston.

Also, in the nineteenth century, interest in development psychology was started. In 1891, Stanley Hall (1844-1924) established the first journal specialized in the development in the United States of America. In 1896 Wetmer established the first psychological clinic for under-developed children in Philadelphia (in the United States).

Title of the first educational psychological was called on Edward Thorndike who published the first book entitled (Educational Psychology) in 1903.

In 1910, the first journal of educational psychology was established. The first article in the first edition of the journal was by (Thorndike), where he promised that educational psychology will provide valuable contribution to education.

In 1913-1914, Thorndike published (Educational Psychology) in three volumes that include reports of all almost psychological studies that have a relationship with education. In cooperation with his colleagues and students in the Faculty of Education in Columbia University, Thorndike provided fundamental contributions in studying intelligence and measuring intellectual abilities, in teaching mathematics, algebra, vocabulary and reading, and in how to move the effect of learning from one attitude to another. Furthermore, he developed an important theory in learning in the method of linking stimulants with responses. Then the theory developed afterwards by others to become the theory of procedural conditional learning of high scientific benefit.

One of the prominent features in the field of educational psychology is the book wrote by William James (1842-1910) entitled (Talks to Teachers).

By the end of the nineteenth century, interests in applying the principles of the new science in the field of education were started. In 1888, the National Educational Association in the United States had decided to consider educational psychology as a necessary and required subject in preparing the teacher.

Thus, the conditions were ripe with the beginnings of the twentieth century to start educational psychology as a major specialization in universities. Three academic positions of professionship specialized in this field held by three of the pioneers: Edward Lee Thorndike (187-1949), Charles H. J. and Lewis M. Truman (1877-1956). From among these pioneers, Thorndike is especially considered the father of this science; he spent all his professional time as a professor to this subject in the Faculty of Teachers in Columbia University from 1899 to 1949.

Then, many of the scientists leaders started to visit the field of educational psychology and its subjects until it clearly specified in 1920. Where works and researches followed in succession, laboratories were established, specialized journals were published and conferences were held which contributed in specifying the nature of this science.

As for the extent of the interests of the Arab World in educational psychology, interest in psychology in general and in educational psychology in particular was limited on Egypt in the early thirties when the Education Institute for Teachers (Faculty of Education in Ein Shams University today) and pilot schools were established. Ismail Al-Qabbani and Professor Abdul Aziz A Qosi were of the pioneers of this movement, whose leadership was attributed to them. Then this movement developed by the second generation represented by Said Khairi, Mohammad Abdul Salam Ahmad, Ra'afat Naseem, Ahmad Saleh Zaki and Faud Al Bahi Alsayed, and their followers, all of them were interested in issues of psychometrics, individual differences, learning and training. They had participated in many of the educational programs that built on psychological basics. They have their contributions in the field of education. Development still exists by the new generation.

Development of Education Psychology

As we mentioned, the image of educational psychology started to be determined in the beginning of 1920. Most of the psychologists were optimistic regarding their future, where their works were prospered in the progressive education and scientific education movement.... Until 1930 when the Great Depression began to spread in America and doubt in science and technology began with it, scientific and educational efforts were subsided and educational psychology had took a humble position for its accomplishments and possibilities in developing education.

The situation remains as it is until a group of factors occurred which had a significant effect in making changes on all scientific and educational levels, including educational psychology. Foremost among these factors: The Second World War, having number of children after war, development of educational curriculum movement and taking care of disadvantaged children.

Many of psychologists had worked in the fields of armed forces during the Second World War. They had to search for solutions for many practical educational problems resulted from war and when war ended they transformed to work in fields of education.

Having a large number of children contributed in developing the field of psychology especially in schools, where the need for educational psychologists occurred to select educational materials, to prepare training and evaluation programs, and to conduct educational tests.

As for the interest of efforts in developing and upgrading education curricula, educational psychologists along with specialists in science and mathematics had contributed to provide new curricula, and had developed new programs to prepare the teacher, which accompany these advanced and developed curricula.

As for the national interest in disadvantaged students, educational psychologists tended to evaluate programs that achieve the desired instructional objectives.

Social forces led to rapid growth in number of specialists in the field of educational psychology between 1960 and 1980 in particular, while cooperation between education and psychology had received support as a result of the emergence of procedural psychology. The fifties and sixties witnessed large interest in programmed education. Social and scientific interests led during this period to work on improving the education system in the United States which led to the progress of educational researches and development. Educational Psychologists found in the educational applications a reasonable test for their learning work. New clear and certain trends occurred in the educational psychology, where a book in 1964 was wrote on learning and education theories. Such book issued by the National Association for Studying Education. This book includes several chapters wrote by senior psychologists. It is clear in this book the prevalence of applied nature on the topics of educational psychology.

Fifth: Research Methods in Educational Psychology

1- Research Strategy in Educational Psychology:

Talking about research approaches in educational psychology brings us to the question posed by the American psychologist Ausubel about what research strategy in this science is and it is a theoretical or applied science?

In the context of answering this question, we find that educational psychology is a theoretical and applied science at the same time; it is theoretical because it seeks to discover knowledge and organize it by scientific organized ways, and it is applied because it aims to apply its data and other data of psychology on solving educational problems in the classroom.

In this particular subject, each of Dr. Muhi Edden Touq and Dr. Abdul Rahman Adam emphasize that it can not be said that there are pure theoretical or pure applied studies. The reason is what seems theoretical now may enter into application after few years; also there are no applied studies without starting from theoretical background in one way or another. Such way seems exactly right regarding education and educational psychology.

In agreement with these data, Dr. Touq and Dr. Adas mention a proposal for the scientist (Hiligard-1964) that implies to the presence of a continuous series of researches, which one of its parts dominates the pure theoretical research and the other part dominates the applied research. Hiligard finds, regarding the development of learning studies, six types of studies in this series that can be determined as follows:

a) Learning researches that did not take into consideration the adequacy of results of educational attitudes and used animal organisms as individuals in the study, for example studying animal learning in mazes.

b) Learning researches that use human beings as individuals but conducted in laboratories without taking into consideration the application of results on class learning, for example verbal learning studies-learning meaningless chains and sections-in psychology laboratories.

c) Learning researches conducted by using students selected in psychology laboratories and by using some studying materials without taking into consideration the adaptation of this type of learning to class learning, for example the study of effectiveness of programmed education for learning English as an example in psychology laboratories.

d) Learning researches by using students selected in experimental classes in schools and by using teachers selected with certain specifications and trained for experiment purposes, for example conducting studies from the previous type (c) in school.

e) Learning researches that aim in applying the results of studies in the previous level (d) on regular classes by using regular teachers.

f) Learning researches that start from the regular class attitude and in the normal circumstance of the school, and aim to solve some educational problems in it.

The three first types of researches can be considered to be more pure theoretical researches or the last three researches to be more applied researches, all of which constitute the theoretical and applied studies in educational psychology.

2- Research Methods in Educational Psychology:

Some argue that despite the expansions occurring in the methods and approaches of scientific research, research in human sciences, including educational psychology, did not receive the progress that natural sciences received such as chemistry and physics, whether in terms of concepts, principles and generalizations used in these sciences or in terms of methods and approaches followed therein.

The reason may be in falling human sciences behind natural sciences is the difference in the nature of phenomena that these sciences consider. Complexity of phenomena, concepts and relationships that human sciences include makes its treatments more difficult than the treatment of phenomena and concepts of natural sciences. However, complexity of human phenomena does not mean the impossibility of its research necessarily, yet it makes this research more difficult and complex.

Nevertheless, these difficulties did not prevent standing on some of the basic concepts and principles that educational psychology uses in explaining the behavioral phenomena of strong relationship with the educational-learning status, in order to understand, control and predict it.

3- Concepts in Educational Psychology:

Concepts used in fields of educational psychology refer to aspects of human behavior. Such aspects transfer to educational activity and merged in it. Concepts also refer to aspects of environment that links with this behavior.

Concepts may take the image of variables or dimensions in which this changing or difference occurs among individuals or environmental events. The meaning of concept depends on its definition from one hand, and on methods used in its study or measuring the variable opposite to it. Educational psychology deals with number of concepts related to it as well as it deals with physics, chemistry, biology and physiology with special concepts for each.

Concepts of educational psychology are characterized by diversity and variety. Some of which are wide and comprehensive such as intelligence, learning, tendency, attitude and motivation …. etc, which prevents them from determining accurately. Some are less comprehensive, more specific and clearer such as response, enhancement, movement and stimuli ….. etc.

It should be noted that many concepts of educational psychology are only assumptions that researchers had to set them to explain a certain behavioral phenomenon that connected with the education-learning process. Motivation, for example, is an assumption that researches had to create when they face the problem of explaining differences existing among individuals in terms of performance in a certain field in case of the similarity of other conditions or factors that may affect in this performance. Therefore, researches attribute differences in performance to differences in motivation.

It is common to use the term (variables) to indicate the concepts of educational psychology. The reason in using these terms is the difference in individuals in terms of the nature of these concepts; they differ in the motivation level, in intelligence ratios and in the ability of learning and remembering …. etc. Also, the reason of using is attributed to changes that may occur on the individual himself as a result of growth factors, maturity, experience and the difference in the nature of the environment; therefore concepts (change) as a result of difference occurring among individuals and as a result of (their changing), which led to using (variables) to refer and indicate to concepts of educational psychology.

4- Principles in Educational Psychology:

Educational psychology goes beyond concepts to principles that include relationships between concepts that take the image of generalizations. These opinions remain as hypotheses until supported by methods of scientific research. If evidences on their validity were available they will transformed and become scientific laws.

These scientific laws (or relationships between concepts, variables or dimensions) are not only a subject for definition or observation as the case in logics or mathematics, but they must be examined imperically (as hypotheses), i.e. they must be derived depending on the word of experience. This is true on educational psychology, as an imperical science, that accepts a relationship between concepts, variables or dimensions, i.e. (hypothetically) as scientific principle or scientific law if this relationship agrees with experience facts, as determined by data or information collected by the researcher regularly.

In the context of the concepts and principles of educational psychology, this science seeks to achieve three aims, namely: understanding, prediction and control. They are aims that human being tried to achieve from the beginning of thinking in natural phenomena surrounded by him. He seeks from the beginning to explain these phenomena and know its reasons, as he tried to predict it in the future. He expressed his wish in controlling them. This is educational psychology, as other science; it tries to achieve these aims through searching phenomena that falls within the field of his interest.

Unit Two

Instructional Objectives

Content:

- Concept of Instructional Objectives and its Resources

- Levels of Instructional Objectives

- Behavioral Objectives and its Components

- Dimensions of Behavioral Objectives

- Formulation of Behavioral Objectives

First: a- Concept of Instructional Objectives and its Resources

The concept of the word (objectives) takes two kinds or trends of meanings:
One of them identifies the objectives concepts as being general educational aims, and the other identifies them as being instructional objectives.

This distinction between (Educational aims) and (Instructional objectives) has a special importance in educational psychology. The term educational aims indicate the broad and wide aims and the prevailing values in the educational system, which are usually determined by education philosophers. While instructional objectives suggest the patterns of qualitative performance acquired by students through different education methods.

To further identify the concept of objective term in its right frame, we rather address the meaning of educational aims in detail and in general.

The Meaning of Educational Aim

John Dewey says in the meaning and content of the aim: "the aim indicates the result of any natural work on the consciousness level. In other word it means managing consequences from its possible results arising from a conduct, in a certain situation and by a certain way, and to benefit of what is expected to direct observation and experience."

Thus, the aim is an organized and ordered work. This work includes a group of studied steps. Every step must lead to the next step in order this work reaches its peak or end.

In order for this work to reach the desired end, it must be based on a deep knowledge of the possible end and the means that help in achieving it. "When the human being who is doing a work thinks in the result of his work, thinks intelligently in the steps of this work, relates between the steps in light of his expectations of the result, in light of his previous experiences, and what he is doing of adjusting work steps according to his perception of its relation and sequence in a way he notices safety of these steps, his motive to this work becomes an aim."

Achieving aims requires that the educational work passes by several steps. First of these steps is to crystallize, arrange and organize these aims so as to become less general and more specific. Then follows choosing modes and means that help in achieving these aims. Finally these aims must be translated into definite ends that are easy to achieve and measure, such as behavioral, cognitive and motor purposes that teachers seek to achieve in their students.

It seems from what we have presented about the meaning of the educational aim that there is a strong relationship between this aim and the human behavior. This relationship becomes clear when looking to learning as scientism that includes all types of experiences to reach desired educational results. That education is happening when the student is subject to a complete experience where there is work and activity or knowledge and assignment. Also, in the experience there is the fulfillment of this assignment so as this experience change his behavior. Learning in this meaning changes the personality of the individual so that it can not be said that he has learned unless his look to things changes, his behavior is modified and he is more able to handle environment and live in it.

Within the limits of this meaning, most definitions of the science encounter, which confirm the connection between the educational aims and behavioral modifications, where we find that Gates defines science as "a change in behavior that has the feature of continuity or the feature of making frequent efforts in order for the individual to reach a response that satisfy his motives and achieves his ends."

Mursell defines learning as "including continuous improvement in performance. The nature of this improvement could be observed as a result of changes that occur during learning". In this definition what refer to the behavioral changes that occur due to learning.

Guil Ford defines learning as "a change in behavior that occurs as a result of stimulation."

Perhaps in these definitions – definitions of (Gates, Mursell and Guil Ford) what explains the true state of affairs of learning process; since it changes the behavior of the individual (or the organism) we can measure as a result of the improvement in his performance. These definitions also explain a number of basic conditions in the learning process and the factors affecting it, such as the importance of motives existence, the importance of making kinds of activity to reach these educational aims in addition to the importance of understanding relationships included in the educational situation.

The relationship circle between the educational aims and behavioral changes becomes clear if we knew that learning for which such aims were placed is a psychological or behavioral phenomenon in itself that exemplifies in the organism changing his behavior such as his response to certain internal or external stimuli.

b- Resources of Aims

When building and forming educational aims, their creators must stop at some resources so as to study and analyze it and to recognize its demands and needs, in order that the educational aims are suitable with the needs of these resources, because it is difficult to build successful educational aims without getting to know the resources from which these aims must be derived. When deriving aims, we must look at these resources comprehensively. Do not concentrate on one resource and skip one or more aspect of these resources, because much negativity will result from the partial look. For example, focusing only on the nature of the individual may lead to confirming individualism at the expense of socialism. Also, focusing on the society culture and ignoring the era's culture will lead to solidity of culture in that society.

While paying attention to the era's culture, without taking into consideration the circumstances and nature of society will lead to ignoring values and morals of the society. This will lead to society loss of its identification and personality. For this we should, when deriving aims, look at these resources from which educational aims are derived with an overall look, and dispose of the partial look that leads to the rise of many educational problems.

We will try to briefly indicate the most important resources that must be observed when building educational aims:

Society: is the first of the resources that must be observed when deriving aims

Every society of human societies has its own culture, its past, present and future, its political, economic and social range, its values, customs and traditions. It is necessary that education aims of any society flow out from the culture of this society, in order to be characterized by originality, to win the trust of the society members, to be able to contribute in achieving the society objectives and to participate in its development and advancement. There are certain matters concerning society. Educational aims creators must observe it. Of these matters is the following:

- Educational aims creators must look at society with a comprehensive look. This look is not restricted to one of life aspects in the society and ignores the other, such as paying attention to the past of the society and ignoring its present and future.

- They must review and study society's culture, in order to be able to realize the good and bad cultural elements. Then they have to make the educational process works for the support and continuation of the good cultural elements, and for fighting bad elements.

The successful education in old and recent times was such education that relates to the society and attempts to help it to achieve its objectives, ends and higher ideals.

1- Nature of the individual

This resource is related to understand the nature of the human being. As long as the human being is the subject matter of education, which is the basic core that the educational process must focus on, then when deriving educational aims you must choose the aims that fulfill the individual ego, cultivate his personality from its different aspects, and match with the student needs and his innate motives and acquired habits.

That might necessitate for creators of educational aims the availability of many studies concerning the development of the individual and the characteristics of such development. Such information shall be used when deriving the educational aims-then the educational process could construct-aims, methods and styles-a construction that fit the students needs and characteristics of their development, and be compatible with their tendencies and readiness. This will lead that the educational process becomes more effective for students as it will work to stimulate their desires and motivate their interests. No doubt there is a difference between the attitude of the student who wants the learning of a subject he feels its importance and the need to learn it, and another student who learns a lesson he feels it was imposed on him without feeling its importance or why he is learning it. The more the educational work could stimulate the interests, tendencies and desires of the students, the more they will become responsive to learning.

Perhaps we conclude from this saying that understanding the nature of the individual is from the important resources that must be taken into account when deriving the educational aims. Creators of aims must be aware of the studies that tackled explanation of the individual's nature, which studied characteristics of human development in its different stages, then using such information carefully when building aims, in order that educational work fits the nature of the individual.

2-   Era's culture

This is the third resource that must be observed when deriving educational aims. Creators of educational aims must recognize the nature of the contemporary culture and realize its characteristics, advantages and styles, in order to create a contemporary culture that could proceed in conformity with progress and development and do not lean toward civilizational retardation.

These are the resources of educational aims in general. While the organized instructional objectives are taken from the following resources listed according to its generality then to the most specific:

1-   The board lines of curriculum included in the philosophy of education, which include the general objectives of study (educational policy).

2-   The curriculum contents (the curriculum in a material)

Second: Levels of Instructional Objectives

Each of Krathwohl, D. R & Pyne suggest classification of instructional educational objectives levels into three categories, which are:

1-   The general level (the general objectives):

Objectives in this level are more abstract, general and comprehensive. In this level the final outcome of a complete educational process is described, or the wide range objectives that the important training and educational program seeks to, such as the curriculum of the secondary school, elementary education or university education. This level is the one which the description of educational aims is applied. Examples of these aims:

* The development of religious and ethical values.

* The development of basic skills in reading, writing and mathematics.

* The development of citizenship by acquiring information, skills and trends related to the national and political issues, the nation and the era in which the student lives, and using it in working to improve society conditions.

* Learning the social role suitable for the student's gender (male, female).

* Preparing the student professionally so as to be qualified to perform a certain work after graduation.

2-   The intermediate level:

It is a less abstract and more specified level than the previous level, in which the comprehensive general objectives are transformed into qualitative behavior that determine potentials of the final performance that comes out of students who succeed in learning a specific unit of the school curriculum, in a complete curriculum, or in a group of educational curricula. This is the level to which description of educational objectives is applied.

When this applies to the elementary school for example, we find that the aim of developing the basic skills in reading and writing (by eliminating math) could be analyzed to more accurate and specific aims.

3-   The special level:

It is the complete detailed level of the educational aims, in which these aims are defined more qualitative, specified and detailed so as to become a guide to prepare and select learning materials and evaluation after that. This level is the level to which description of educational tasks (or works or demands) is applied.

Take for example from the aims of the intermediate level the aim of: naming the alphabetic letters. We can derive from this aim more qualitative aims for the third level in this respect, which describe the set of tasks, demands or works such as the students ability to distinguish between the similar letters which could be easily mixed up such the letters (ث،ت،ب), the two letters (ش،س), the letters (ج،ح،خ), the two letters (ق،ف), the two letters (ز،ذ) and so on. This special qualitative aim leads to choosing the learning subject in which the child could be trained to recognize these letters separately or to choose from it when it is displayed together.

In fact, in determining the instructional educational objectives we need these three levels. Defining on the general (first) level has its almost importance in the delivery of education aims to the public and to reach a kind of common public understanding of what the education seeking to achieve.

However, to achieve the educational aims at this level alone is not sufficient. We might agree for example that the education aim is "to prepare the good citizen" but it is difficult to agree on what this big aim includes, meaning of citizenship might differ from a society to another. Yet it might differ according to types of interests of different groups of which the one society consists. When this difference occurs, this means that the abstract general term might lead to different educational ways, each of them may be described differently at the most qualitative levels in determining aims.

To achieve a sufficient amount of agreement about the educational aims, we need to translate such aims to the second (intermediate) level or the level of objectives, which might be called the level of reinforcing transition aims. Then after that we can translate the sub aims into behavioral procedural elements in the third level, or the level of demands or tasks.

Here we should determine the overall volume of behavior patterns in detail. Thus this could be called the level of mastery aims, because it requires from the student to master all of the behavior patterns or a sample of it in a complete degree of proficiency. Examples of mastery aims are memorization of multiplication table, to memorization of poetry for Abi Tammam or distinction between types of motives.

In fact, the process of determining educational aims requires a continuous review. Where each level helps in understanding the other levels and each progress we achieve in one of the levels has its direct effects in the lower and higher levels. The researcher could reach a degree of accuracy in understanding the educational aims if he uses this method by progressing forward and returning backward between the different aims levels.

Third: Behavioral Objectives and its Components

One of the educational definitions is a definition that education is a process by which we mean to make desired changes in the students' behavior, i.e., changes in what they think or the ways by which they work or feel. These changes in the behavior is expressed in the image of what is expected from the student to be able to do at the end of studying the curriculum, or a number of lessons, is what is called the behavioral objectives.

Thus, the behavioral objective describes the educational achievement or the final behavior of the learner, more than describing the means used to reach this behavior. Therefore, the behavioral objectives require the use of words or verbs that refer to performance or work such as: read, write, describe, count … etc.. While words or verbs that refer to (an implied) verb such as: understand, think, estimate and evaluate … etc., cannot be considered behavioral objectives because of the impossibility to notice it. The process of (thinking), (understanding) or (evaluation) cannot be noticed unless it was translated into behavioral terms and apparent performance that could be noticed, measured and evaluated.

The good behavioral objective is the one that reaches the end for which it was placed and succeeded in delivering the educational intention to the reader, whether this reader was the creator of the objective himself, the learner, or any other external reader. The more the objective or the behavioral term was successful in demonstrating the successful learner image and conveying it to others, so as to become similar to the image created by the creator of the objective himself, the more the objective was successful, helpful and able to guide the educational-learning process. The best objectives and most effective and efficient, are those that enable the teacher or who in charge of the educational affairs to take the biggest possible number of decisions related to its measurement, achievement and evaluation, which are characterized by the biggest possible number of identification and clarity, and eliminate any form of ambiguity, misunderstanding, or explanation. But, how can we formulate this type of behavioral objectives? And what are the components of the behavioral objective that enable the learner to formulate objectives marked with usefulness and the possibility of delivering it to the learner easily and clearly?

Components of Behavioral Objectives

The basic components of the behavioral objectives are determined as follows:

1-   The apparent performance and behavior of the learner:

This component indicates the desired and precise behavior, which will define the change that will happen to the learner's behavior after finishing teaching a certain educational unit so that identification is evident, precise and explicit. This identification concentrates in the first place on the final behavior of the learner or what is called (the behavioral outputs).

Performance usually refers to any activity performed by the learner, or this performance might be apparent and noticeable by eyesight, such as writing, drawing and written correction, or by hearing, such as reading loudly or reciting. This activity might also be implied and unnoticeable by eyesight or hearing, such as the intellectual mathematical operations or thinking. However, the successful behavioral phrase is able to identify what the learner must do when it becomes clear that he mastered the objective. As the teacher is already unable to know what is going in the learner's (mind) to understand his knowledge and trends, thus he has to (conclude) these (inner) operations.

This kind of conclusion is not achieved unless it was based on what the learner say or do. In other expression, these conclusions must be based on the verbal or motor behavior of the learner. The teacher can often reach it by the direct observation of the desired teaching outcomes.

The teacher cannot know the success and achievement of his objectives except by observing his students acting in a way, or doing something to express these abstract cases. Thus, the most important feature of the behavioral objective at all, is the feature that clearly determines and describes the quality of performance that the learner must do.

A behavioral phrase such as "the student realizes the importance of the climate in agriculture" does not satisfy the desired purpose, because it does not determine the behavior, or the desired performance to manifest whether the student had actually (realized) this importance. Therefore, the teacher must translate the word (realize) into a behavioral verb that the student can perform and the teacher is able to observe and measure, such as saying "the student has to explain the relationship between the climate and the plants" and "to demonstrate the diversity of plants according to the diversity of climate." These two phrases are clearer than the previous one, because they are more specified to what the student has to do, and because words such as "explain" or "demonstrate" are more able to determine the apparent noticeable and measurable behavior than the word "realize". However, were the specifications of good behavioral objective achieved by that identification? The objective still needs more clarification and identification, because the previous two phrases did not indicate the conditions and circumstances of performance, i.e. they didn't refer to the second component of the behavioral objective.

2-   Conditions of performance:

This component refers to the conditions or circumstances through which the final behavior of the learner appears, which must be available when doing the performance. The process of defining the final behavior is insufficient to prevent misunderstanding or the variety and diversity of explanations. Hence, the behavioral objective takes more obvious form when the teacher sets some conditions that define the circumstances and the context of performance, such as allowing or not allowing the use of maps, dictionaries, atlases, school books, calculators or logarithmic tables… etc.

But does the behavioral objective takes its best form merely by defining the behavior and its conditions? To limit these two components prevents the right process of the change required to be created in the learner behavior. Therefore, we must define an acceptable performance level that could be taken as a criterion for success and as considering it evidence to the attainment and achievement of the objective, which is the third component of the behavioral objective.

3-   The acceptable performance level:

This component is characterized by the quality of the required performance. Such quality shows whether the learner had mastered the objective or not. The performance level must be determined clearly that enable the teacher to recognize the acceptable response, as determining a certain percentage of the correct relations or responses. The behavioral objective that says: "the student must be able to solve algebra equations of first degree by referring to similar equations and using the calculator" does not achieve all features of the good behavioral objective. It is necessary to identify a specific performance criterion that could be referred to in order to recognize the learner's success in achieving the objective, such as saying: "The student must correctly solve seven equations out of ten."

Consequently, the behavioral objective becomes more clearer, specific, accurate and effective, because it describes the behavior required to be performed by procedural phrases that can be observed and measured, and because it identifies the performance conditions of this behavior that control it and influence the variables that affect it. This behavior also put an acceptable performance level that indicates the extent to which the educational end is attained and achieved.

Fourth: Dimensions of Behavioral Objectives

In the context of the educational aims, educational psychologists had reached approaches by which the behavioral objectives dimensions are determined. These approaches help teachers to think of objectives alternates and the methods of its determination.

Educational psychology explains from its part three dimensions or classifications of the behavioral objectives which are the following with its respective domains:
First dimension: Cognitive objectives and its intellectual-cognitive domain.
Second dimension: Emotional objectives and its sentimental-emotional-affective domain.
Third dimension: Psychomotor objectives and its psychomotor domain.

A fourth dimension is also added. This dimension includes the domain of objectives classification according to education types.

Educational psychology had demonstrated ways of defining objectives in the framework of these domains by using structures consisting of behavior and its subject matter. These efforts emerged as a result of concentrated works made by a group of scientists and those interested in psychometrics and educational testing, on top of them is Benjamin Bloom in the period between 1948-1953, where they examined and analyzed the educational aims for different educational materials taught in the American academic institutes and faculties as a preliminary step toward reclassifying them. The following is a demonstration of the efforts made to classify the behavioral objectives and defining its types, exemplified by the aforementioned three types and its domains, in addition to the field of objectives classification according to learning types.

First dimension: Cognitive objectives and its intellectual-cognitive domain, (Bloom's pyramid in objectives):

Bloom's taxonomy of the educational aims in the intellectual-cognitive domain was issued in 1956, in a pyramid order for objectives. This order includes six levels relating to different cognitive processes, or the intellectual behavior in terms of recalling and recognizing information and developing intellectual skills. This order extends from the simple to the compound as illustrated in the following figure:

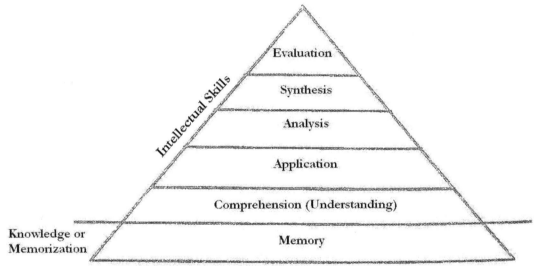

A figure that illustrates objectives levels in the intellectual – cognitive domain

It becomes obvious from this figure that Bloom's taxonomy includes two large main categories: Knowledge or memorization category that relates to recalling information and cognitions stored in the memory, and the intellectual skills category that includes five levels: Comprehension or understanding, application, analysis, synthesis and evaluation.

The following is some of explanations for the categories of this taxonomy and for the levels of each of them.

First: Knowledge (memory) category:

As we had mentioned, it is the category that denotes recalling information and cognition stored in the memory as a result of previous learning. It is recalled by providing the learner with some of the contexts that facilitate recalling process so as recalling becomes effective. This category is divided into the following subcategories:

1- Knowledge of details or qualitative specifications: By this we mean recalling information units in a detailed separated sub-image. In spite that this category lies in the lowest levels of which the cognitive intellectual pyramid consists, yet it forms the elements of which the most complex and abstract intellectual activity images consist. This category is divided by its turn into two divisions:

   a) Knowledge of symbols and terms of the educational material, such as the term of poetry and prose or the subject and the predicate.

   b) Knowledge of qualitative facts (detailed information) related to a subject, such as names of some important literary or historical characters, multiplication tables, reading, drawing, dancing or playing on a musical instrument... etc.

2- Knowledge of ways and means: meaning to know the ways of collecting and organizing this detailed information. It is divided into the following:

   a) Knowledge of traditions prevailing in the educational material and its rules, such as syntax rules, mathematical operations rules or traffic rules... etc.

   b) Knowledge of relations, operations and effects (outcomes): These refer to operations or movements of time progression such as slavery liberation movement or people's movements, women's struggle for equality or the different social reformation movements ... etc.

   c) Knowledge of the classifications and categories to which the phenomena of the educational material are divided, such as climax types, poetry forms and behavior patterns... etc.

   d) Knowledge of criteria used to judge the validity of opinions, principles, facts or images of activity included in the educational material, such as the criteria of judging a piece of literature or a work of art, recreational activity, or economic, social, psychological or scientific theory… etc.

e) Knowledge of research and study methods in a certain domain. This means knowing the basics of scientific method and approaches and techniques of scientific research that the learner must know when researching or handling a certain educational material, such as ways of using libraries or registering bibliographies, collecting and classifying data, handling variables or ways of statistical processing.

3- Knowledge of generalities and abstractions: This means knowing the main ideas around which phenomena are organized addressed by a certain domain. This category is divided into the following:

a) Knowledge of principles, generalities and rules prevailing in the educational material, such as gravity principle, principles of genetics, learning principles and principle of supply and demand …etc.
b) Knowledge of general intellectual theories and structures such as relatively theory, learning and assessment theory and economic and mathematical theories.

Second: Category of Intellectual Skills

It is the second basic category of the classification categories; it is what bloom call Intellectual Skills in which he refers to the general ways in working and dealing with the educational material. These skills are divided into five basic categories each of which is divided into a number of subcategories as follows:

1- Comprehension (Understanding)

This level represents the most common intellectual skills categories in education. This might be because of several reasons relating to the components of the educational process as a whole, such as objectives, methods, school books, ways of teaching, means and types of school tests and the ways adopted in educational testing and evaluation. This category consists of three subcategories, namely:

a) Alteration or translation: It is exemplified in interest and accuracy in which certain information is altered from one formula to another. Translation is usually judged by the degree of demand and accuracy, that is to what limit the main ideas are kept in the origin although its image has changed. Translation takes different forms, such as alteration from one level of abstraction to another, or translation from a symbolic or verbal form to another.

b) Interpretation: It is mean the ability to explain or summarize information, which is the ability must be available in the learner in order to be able to reorganize, demonstrate and illustrate ideas included in a certain educational material, or summarize it.

c) Extrapolation: It means to reach estimations, expectations or predictions depend on understanding trends, tendencies, conditions or states described by the content. It may also include reaching conclusions about the content implications. Extrapolation may also include judgments about the overall origin that content is considered a sample of it, or about the sample when the content describes a general overall origin.

2- Application

Application in (Bloom's) taxonomy means the use of abstractions in new situations. These abstractions may be general ideas image, work rules, principles or theories. In order for the application level achieves the desired objective, the educational situation related to it must have two basic features, first: the problematic nature of the situation, that is the learner must face problems that require solution, and the second: novelty or unfamiliarity, that is the context that has the application must be different from the contexts in which information desired to be used were learned.

3- Analysis

Analysis means to divide content into its elements or parts of which it consists so that the pyramid order of ideas and meanings or relationships between ideas becomes clear. This category is divided into:

a) Analysis of elements: that is to define elements of which the content consists, whether these element were expressly drafted (such as assignments and outcomes) or not expressly drafted (such as hypotheses or phrases that denote a fact, a value, an intent or an opinion).

b) Analysis of relationships: it means the analysis of basic relations between the content elements or its different parts, such as the relation between assignments and evidence, between assignments and outcomes or between different kinds of evidence.

c) Analysis of principles: this is the most complicated level of analysis, since it requires handling and organizing content structure. This includes basics, principles, points of views, trends and values that make the content an overall unit.

4- Synthesis

Synthesis means to combine between elements and parts so as to form a new overall structure. This includes dealing with units, parts and elements and organizes and relates between them in a way that clearly combine a form or a structure that didn't exist before. This category is divided into:

a) Producing a unique content: meaning to produce ideas and to convey them to others such as writing a story or a piece of prose or poetry.

b) Producing a work plan or project: on the condition that the demands of work, which details are given to the examiner or he gets it by himself (writing a research plan for example), are available in the plan or the project.

c) Producing abstract relations: that is to produce or derive a group of abstract relations in order to classify or explain data or phenomena, and to deduct issues and relations from the group of the main issues.

5- Evaluation

Evaluation means that intellectual process by which the learner makes judgments about the value of the content he is studying. These judgments may be quantitative or qualitative to determine the extent to which the content matches certain criteria. This category is divided into:

a) Judging in light of the internal evidence: It means that to evaluate the extent of the accuracy of the content in light of internal evidence, such as logic accuracy, inner consistency and other inner criteria.

b) Judging in light of exterior criteria: It means to introduce the content in light of criteria from the outside, such as ends, styles or levels, or by comparing between it and other similar contents.

Second dimension: Objectives and its affective domain:

Krathwoht and colleagues issued in 1964 a classification of educational aims in the affective domain. Affective objectives have its importance to educators. This is exemplified in objectives that describe trends, values, tendencies and images of appreciation and harmony. The main problem in this domain was looking for a basic dimension on which the pyramidical affective organization rests, until Krathwoht and colleagues found their desired goal in the (Internalization) concept, which indicates that the process by which behavioral control consistent with what is positively evaluated occurs from within the individual. This means that internalization process is extremely similar to social normalization process. On this basis Krathwoht and colleagues suggest classification of affective objectives into five categories as follows:

1- Receiving-attending

Receiving means the level in which the student is at a degree of sensitivity in the existence of certain phenomena or stimuli, that is he is willing to receive and attend to it. This category is divided into the following:

a) Awareness: It is situated at the lowest levels of temperamental classification. It indicates the awareness of stimuli that provoke the affective behavior, and forms the context in which this behavior occurs.

b) Willingness to receive: It describes the state in which the student distinguishes between the stimulus and other stimuli, and he is willing to attend to it. For example the rigorous attending to the teacher's instructions, or overlooking the individual and collective differences.

c) Stage of controlling attending: Here the student does some positive activity in controlling attending so that he chooses the preferred stimulus and attend to it in spite of the presence of competitive stimulants. For example preferentially attending when reading or hearing a specific poem close to the poet's mood and the meaning he is aiming at or social values prevailing in this poet's era.

2- Responding:

This category includes what is called (interests) objectives which are usually used to denote the willingness that makes the student integrated in a subject, phenomenon or activity so that he feels comfortable when doing or being preoccupied with it. This category is divided into the following:

a) Acquiescence responding: It refers to meanings in obedience and acquiescence where the student shows negativity when starting to behave. Acquiescence term may benefit better than obedience term, where the element responding to suggestion plays big role, and resistance plays less role. The student in this subcategory gives responding, yet he is not accepting the necessity of giving it.

b) Willingness responding: Here it shows the possibility of optional or voluntary behavior. The student commits to give responding not fearing of punishment, but voluntarily.

c) Satisfaction responding: In this level the student is not satisfied with willingness or will, but responding is accompanied with a feeling of comfort and satisfaction, or affective responding that takes the image of feeling of happiness, pleasure or fun.

One of the examples that illustrates this category and its subdivisions is that the student collects pictures of some famous artistic paintings according to the teacher's demand (acquiescence), then he starts looking for models of good art in which elements of shading, perspective, color and design are used thoroughly (willingness), then the student starts playing with clay in making and decorating vessels for the purpose of personal enjoyment and satisfaction.

At this limit the student has distinguished between affective stimuli and started looking for and giving these stimuli an affective denotation and value.

3- Valuation:

It means to give a value or an evaluation for things, phenomena, ideas or behavior patterns. The basic element that distinguishes the behavior here is that it is not forced by the need to acquiescence or obedience, but as a result of the student's commitment to a value or trend. This category is divided into the following subcategories:

a) Acceptance of value: It is a level at which a value is given to phenomenon, thing or behavior, yet it is a stage to show beliefs in some things or different subjects, such as to believe in the importance of mathematics in calculation of a process, or to believe in the value of teaching Arabic literature and its role in provoking the national feeling.

b) Preference of value: In this level the matter goes beyond acceptance and includes bigger amount of commitment by letting it seeks the subjects related to value or trend, for example the willingness to create more friendships and help relationships or the willingness in producing more artistic works… etc.

c) Commitment: This level includes the highest degrees of certainty with regard to belief, trend or value. It is exemplified in loyalty to an issue, principle, objective, group or school in art or literature.

4- Organization:

With the advancement of the student in comprehending values, he may face situations to which more than one value is connected. This requires to organize this value in a value system, or to determine the relationships between them, and to confirm the most prevailing values. This category is divided into the following:

a) Conceptualination: It is a level in which the learner makes intellectual visualization process of values that he must acquire. This process usually starts in formulating values verbally, or in realizing relationships that relate them to the previous values that he believes, such as comparing beliefs with behavior, grasping the morale aspects of personality or distinguishing between theory and practice.

b) Organization of value system: This level refers to behavior patters that the learner shows when his value system is thoroughly balanced, that is when relationships organizing the values are characterized by internal consisting and logical harmony, which indicates a kind of dynamic balance, in which concepts required by the vocational learning interact.

In spite of the difficulties that had been faced in this domain, some scientists felt the importance of educational aims in this domain. Individual attempts appeared for suggesting classifications for these aims. They all considered as a form of scientific hypotheses that need more testing. The domain still waits the emergence of (Bloom's) school taxonomy itself for educational aims in the motor domain.

The first attempt in this track is what was made by R. H. Dave, education professor in Monash University in India, when he discussed in a scientific conference held in Berlin 1968 an imagination of the educational motor aims classification. However, this classification is as a form of scientific hypotheses and needs more research and test to display its validity and efficiency.

Each of Keibler, Barker and Miles made every attempt in putting a classification for objectives in the psychomotor domain based on the sequence of events in development, where they started from two sequences of events.

First sequence: It relates to the development of motor behavior, which usually develops from large gross motor activities, to specialized fine motor activities. This motor sequence is demonstrated in catching process and some additional body movement, to end in the use of only the forefinger and the thumb, and in the development of the child's response to his mother, which begins by using all his body to welcome his mother, and ends in drifting to her, as it is manifested in all the child's movements, such as moving, crawling and walking... etc.

While the second sequence of events is related to the development of communicative behavior, where this behavior usually develops from using the movement or the sign, such as gesture, screaming or crying, to express needs and communicate with others, to use language and speech as a way of communication. After this communicative sequence killer and colleagues describe the psychomotor domain objectives in four basic categories which are:

1- Gross body movements: Objectives here focus on the gross movements of the body. The learner uses his body as a whole when performing some skill, such as jumping, running, throwing the ball or the arrow and swimming. The learner's ability is usually measured by the speed by which he performs such movements (running, swimming) or its force (throwing the spear or the ball, jumping ... etc) so that new values are generated from this interaction, or value compositions with a higher abstract level as developing some criteria to evaluate some works of art or finding some justifications to justify the value of morals role in public life.

5- Characterization by Value

At this level comprehension and organization processes reach the stage in which the individual responds with a coordinated response to the situations loaded with values.

And at this level behavior is made without provoking emotions unless the individual was in a threatening or challenging situation. This category is divided into the following:

a) Generalized set: It means to generalize the control process of the student's behavior so that the student could be described and characterized as a person through the controlling general tendencies called by different names such as the specific inclination, orientation towards phenomena or the advanced willingness to work in a certain way.

b) Characterization: This level refers to the group of general final objectives in which the learner acquires in the affective-sentimental domain, which make him a unique person, so that his beliefs, trends, tendencies, readiness and values are integrated in a comprehensive overall philosophy that characterizes his life and marks it with a distinguished characteristic, such as humanity, charity or romance … etc.

Third dimension: Psychomotor objectives and its psychomotor domain.

Bloom indicated in 1956 a third domain of the domains to which educational aims are classified-beside cognitive and affective domains- This domain is called psychomotor domain, which relates to the activity of handling, taking, motor and muscular skills and muscular neural synergy. Bloom drew attention to the difficulty of such domain especially because the decrease in the objectives related to it whether in secondary or university education.

This psychomotor domain is concerned with objectives related to manual handling, motor skills and sensory-motor synergy, such as writing, speaking, drawing, handicrafts, playing on musical instruments, exercises of physical education, dancing, artistic works and skills.

1- Finally coordinated movements: This category addresses the fine movements that the learner must acquire to perform a certain skill, such as the movement of the hand, fingers and eye that requires certain exercises to master. The learner's ability in this domain is measured by the extent to which he achieves mastery in performing the required skill.

2- Non verbal communication groups: Objectives of this category belong to what is called sign language or movements, where it refers to the learner's ability to communicate with others without using speech, such as expressive movements manifested on the face to denote a specific psychological state, such as thinking, or fear and anger, gesture movements that express some events, or aesthetical movements such as the one used in ballet or dancing on ice … etc.

3- Speech behavior: Objectives of this category belong to speech communication behavior, where the learner uses speech to communicate with others. The learner's ability becomes in this domain in speech performance that expresses meaning, such as the clear pronunciation, voice intonation or slow recitation, such as performing interrogative, condemnative, sentimental or oratorical tone … etc. Objectives of this category usually relate to the theatrical performance, learning foreign language or learning different dialects … etc.

Fourth dimension: Classification of objectives according to learning types:

Classifications of the previous objectives were based on a private point of view, where its attention core was directed to the human aspects materialized in his behavioral activities, with respect to being recalls, knows, thinks, loves and hates and comprehends several trends and values. He also moving and using his body and muscles, so objectives classifications came in light of the nature of these domains that form each of the cognitive, affective motor domain.

On other hand, we fine psychologists address education from a different angle. From among these psychologists are Miller, Coleman and Gagne'e, who said that there are more than one kind of instruction, each of which controls different conditions and principles. This means that there are different behavioral patterns, which are acquired through different educational patterns. In light of this point of view, Gagne'e (1965) puts eight patterns for education that take pyramidical sequential form, the objectives could be classified according to it, namely:

1- Signal Learning: It is a learning that includes emotional responses acquired according to the law of classical conditioning. We bring to mind here Pavlov experiment as the best example of this educational pattern. This learning is not limited only to animals, but many of behavioral responses of the human being are acquired in this way. Happiness response provoked by seeing the mother, frowning response provoked by seeing the ruthless teacher, and the worry response provoked by the exam, all of these are examples of this kind of learning that could be used in some class situations, where some educational materials are conditioned by the emotional responses of teachers. The word (earthquake) for example provokes several different emotional responses in students such as fear, anger, sadness or mercy and sympathy … etc. Therefore, some of special information of earthquake is linked to this kind of responses which makes it easy to learn and remember.

2- Stimulus-Response Learning: This type of learning refers to acquiring the ability to make exact responses to a stimulus or specific stimuli, such as the child's response by saying the word "mama" when he sees his mother, not just smiling to her. These responses often receive a certain reward and become rooted to the teacher. This type of learning is applied on the concept of connection of Thorndike. Such concept denotes that the connection between the stimulus and response becomes stronger if it was accompanied or followed by a state of satisfaction-being rewarded. This type of learning can be applied in several educational situations.

3- Chaining Learning: This learning indicates the learner acquiring the ability to connect a sequence of stimulus-response connections. This ability starts in rearranging connections in a right position that leads to achieving the desired behavior or skill.

4- Verbal Anociation Learning: This type of learning is considered a secondary type of chaining. However, connection in it occurs between the connection of stimulus and verbal response. It is manifested in the learner's ability to perform a chain of verbal or linguistic responses that connect between a group of words, syllables or sentences, so that the learner is able to rearrange it in a form, order or pattern that leads to a meaning, which shows the learner's ability to understand relationships existing between those responses, such as the relationship between the word and its meaning, or between words that consist a specific sentence. This type of learning prevails in many different educational materials.

5- Discrimination Learning: This type of learning seems obvious in the learner's ability to discriminate between overlapping group of stimuli, so as he responds to each of these stimuli by a suitable and definite response. The response to see a dog, the word "dog" indicates verbal anociation, whilst the response to every kind of dogs by a response that defines its type and characteristics that discriminate it from other dogs, refers to discrimination learning. This ability to this type of discrimination is important in teaching domain because it enables the learner to respond appropriately.

6- Concept Learning: This learning refers the ability to respond by giving the name or the category to a group of varied stimuli that might differ in its forms, colors, materials, volumes, positions or functions … etc. This kind of learning is made by abstracting one feature or more, that is common between these stimuli, so that common feature or features form a specific concept. The concept of the (ball) for example refers to a group or a category of stimuli that form the balls in the whole world, irrespective of its numbers, colors and volumes. In fact if we knew that most of the words included in the language are a kind of concepts, it will become clear to us the importance of learning the concept and its role in the learning process.

7- Rule Learning: This learning refers to the learner's ability to connect between two or more concepts. The simplest kinds of rules or principles are those that take the following form: "If A happens, B will happen" such as saying: "If we rise above sea level, the atmospheric pressure will decrease". Learning this rule requires understanding several concepts which are the concept of rising and decreasing, the concept of sea level and the concept of atmospheric pressure. Realizing the relationship between these different concepts and connecting between them, and knowing what is reached from this connection of results enable the learner to respond to many other domains, such as the application of this rule or principle in case of rising above sea level or decreasing from it. When the learner reaches this stage, learning becomes verbal because the connections between concepts are originally verbal connections.

8- Problem-Solving Learning: This learning is situated in the highest educational structure that (Gagne'e) talked about. It refers to the learner's ability to use the rules and principles in a chain of behaviors or events that lead to achieving an objective or a problem. Problems might differ in respect of its size, such as the problem of concluding the area of parallelogram depending on knowing the area of the rectangle, or the problem of fighting illiteracy in the Arabian World. Problems also might differ in respect of its importance, such as the problem of organizing the daily activities of the student, or the problem of improving agricultural production, qualitatively and quantitatively. Solving problems usually comes out through new responses or performances made by the learner to reach a solution for a certain problematic situation, by using his previous cognitions, which requires analyzing this situation to the basic principles that shape it by using thinking.

Fifth: Formulation of Instructional Objectives in Behavioral Formulas:

De Cecco thinks that formulating educational instructional objectives in behavioral or procedural formulas is identified in an explicit or implied expression to these events. The explicit expression of these objectives requires identification of the final outcome of learning (or learning outcomes) in light of the performance that could be observed or the apparent behavior. Of course in order to judge that a student has learned, it is inevitable to notice his apparent behavior or performance. The explicit expression of the instructional objective must include these performance styles and not include what cannot be directly observed.

If we wanted to use the classification of variables as it is prevailing in experimental psychology, we say that the explicit formulating instructional objectives must be done in light of the subsidiary variables. These results or final outcomes of teaching are called the final performance.

The following are examples that demonstrate instructional objectives formulated in explicit behavioral formulas in light of the final performance:

- Discrimination between vertebrates and invertebrates.

- Identification of the main systems in the human body.

- Naming the main planets in the solar system.

You have to compare between these explicit procedural behavioral objectives and the list of the following objectives:

- Understanding AL Mutanabbi poetry.

- Taste of modem art.

- Appreciation of the contribution of the Islamic Civilization in the modern civilization.

This last list of the type is what De Cecco calls the implied behavioral formulas of the instructional objectives because the final performance is not explicitly defined, but it is an implied type. All of them denote internal states or hypothetical structures that can not be directly observed.

The difference between the two previous lists of objectives lies in the used "linguistic source". Sources used in the first list of types: discrimination, naming and identification all of these are performance styles that can be observed, while we find that sources in the second list are of the type: understanding, tasting, appreciating all of them are not subject to direct observation.

Of course, the explicit behavioral formulation of educational aims is more obvious than the implied behavioral forms, although the two types have their own value.

On other hand, Dr. Fikri Hassan Rayan identifies the comprehensiveness in formulating objectives. He decides that these formulas are different in respect to its comprehensiveness and expansion. This depends on the purposes for which objectives are made. In this Dr. Rayan mentions a group of formulas for educational aims listed as follows:
- The comprehensive formulas: They imply as a general educational base, and present an image for the objectives at the strong level. These comprehensive objectives are usually an expression of school assignments, which give it certain advantages. These objectives also show the school as an active institution that has an obvious and definite role.

- School grades formulas: Example of these formulas is what mentioned in some curricula that the aim of elementary education is to provide chances of bodily, emotional, intellectual and social development for children by reinforcing emotional stability, to provide chances for healthy life in all times, to provide a healthy environment that provokes bodily and social development and to provide chances of intellectual development for understanding, skills and abilities the human needs in life situations.

- Formulas for certain aspects of the school program: The school program includes different aspects, such as studying in the class, school activity outside the class and services of psychological and social guidance and so on. All these aspects have functions to do in the educational process of the school. It is helpful to make sure that these functions are made effectively. Therefore these formulas are helpful in verifying that every aspect of the program is planned and implemented according to the right educational aims.

- Formulas of educational material or the specific educational domain: Of these examples objectives of social studies or objectives of history material. Formulas are usually detailed since the purpose of such is that the teacher chooses from the objectives mentioned in it what could be achieved in the educational time assigned to students. Objectives are usually formulated in a form of specific educational outcomes such as types of understanding, skills and trends. This formula is beneficial in guiding the educational change for the educational material and its activities.

- Formulas of source and teaching units and subjects: It represents a list of detailed objectives from among which the teacher chooses in commensurate with the circumstances of his students and their school environment.

- Formulas set by students when planning for their work: It is helpful that students of the class set with the guidance of their teacher a formula for their activity objectives in light of the educational material and the school.

Formulas are valued by being obvious and understandable for students, since they write these formulas in their style after discussing it. Such formulas also make them more aware of the purpose of the activities they perform and make their participation in learning process a responsible one.

Unit Three

Intelligence

Content:

- Definition of Intelligence

- Organization of Intelligence and its Theories

- Measurement of Intelligence and its Tests

- Intelligence Determinants

- Using Intelligence Measures in School

Intelligence

Introduction:

In daily life, individuals describe each other as intelligent ones. The student superior in his study is an intelligent student, the physician successful in his career is an intelligent physician, and individual who acts politely in social attitudes is an intelligent individual. Thus, is intelligence the ability to learn, ability to adapt, being successful at work or synthesis of trick? Is the daily use of the concept of intelligence gives an accurate image to its meaning? Can it be taken as a base to classify individuals into different levers? And what will result from this classification as different problems?

In fact, the daily use of the concept of intelligence mostly does not give an accurate image to its meaning. Therefore, its nature and meaning must be clarified by the scientists' attitude and their different trends in explaining and determining its main features.

On other hand, intelligence may be the strongest psychological concepts that link the educational instructional process and with studying in general, which strengthen and confirm the necessity of knowing intelligence from its nature, meaning, definitions, approaches of its measuring and the amount of its linking with school achievement. This could help the teacher in comprehend one of the main factors related to success in school life and in general life, which will pave the road to him for performing his educational task in a more developed and effective way.

Definition of Intelligence

Psychologists were interested in discussing the subject of intelligence. They have scientifically and accurately studied intelligence because it links with behavioral approaches, features of mental activity such as learning and thinking, and stimuli of behavior and its different motives.

Many psychologists tried to define intelligence in short simple phrases through its manifestations. One of these definitions is the following:

- "Intelligence is an organic ability that has a base in physical configuration. The difference in the individuals in it is due to their differences in physical configuration. This ability in this meaning is inherited. This does not mean that intelligence is not affected by environment, instead intelligence is affected by it."

It is obvious that supporters of this definition confirm the genetic factors.

- Binet believes that intelligence is the individual ability to understand, create and direct purposefully to behavior and self-criticism, i.e. the ability of the individual to understand problems and think of its solutions, and measuring or criticizing and adjusting this solution.

- Stern, German scientist, believes that intelligence is the ability to act properly in new attitudes.

- Terman believes that intelligence is the ability of abstract thinking.

- Thorndike believes that intelligence is a group of special independent abilities.

- While Colvin defines intelligence as the ability to learn or ability to achieve. This definition is the most common and it is often used in the school environment.

- Wechsler defines intelligence as the total ability of the individual to purposed work, logic thinking and effective interaction with the environment.

It is clear from these definitions that most of them deal with the individual ability. Nevertheless, we find that there is sort of disagreement on the ability to which these definitions indicate.

From which, Dr. Abdul Majeed Nashwan draws something to the effect that formulation of a simple and comprehensive definition accepted by all psychologists is not an easy thing, where definition varied and differed by difference in concept that form each one of them on the general mental ability.

Sattler attributes the ambiguity of the concept of intelligence and the difficulty precision in identifying it that intelligence is a status not an entity, meaning intelligence does not exist by itself, yet it is a type of description we called on a specific individual when he behaves in a certain way at a certain situation.

While Wesman believes that one of the factors of intelligence ambiguity is that intelligence is the result or outcome of educational experiences of the individual, where intelligence appears as a type of sequence or series of fixed growth functions.

Vernor mentions that ambiguity of the concept of intelligence may be attributed to the diversity and abundance of meanings related to it.

Notwithstanding the ambiguity of the concept of intelligence and the abundance and diversity of its definitions, Dr. Nashwati mentions a limitation to some abilities prevailing in most of the definitions of intelligence, namely:

1- Ability of abstract thinking.

2- Ability of learning.

3- Ability of solving problems.

4- Ability of adaptation and connection with the environment.

It is noticed that all these abilities were integrated in one definition mentioned by Stoddard stating that: "Intelligence is a mental activity in which factors of difficulty, complexion, abstraction, speed, adaptation to reach goal, social value, creation, economy in time and effort are reflected. Intelligence is the ability in continuing in situations that require concentration of mental energy and resistance of emotional factors".

This definition specifies features that must be available in the right measure and aspects that must be taken into consideration when developing intelligence tests.

Organization of Intelligence and its Theories

Intelligence is one of the important subjects discussed since ancient times. It originated in the frame of ancient philosophy then biological and physiological sciences were interested in it which led to be affected by the approaches of such sciences, so it was subject to measurement and experiment. Therefore, scientists were interested in determining its main features.

This is no doubt that interest of various sciences in intelligence indicates that intelligence directly linked with all fields of life. Interest also indicates that intelligence is a process that resulted from interacting different factors that cannot be overlooked and disregarded.

In the context of discussing the nature of intelligence and its organizations, psychologists were interested in two main things:
First: The question whether if our mental abilities (such as awareness, thinking, learning and remembering and other special abilities) are functions of intelligence or if they were relatively or absolutely differentiated?

In other words, the question is whether intelligence is composed of one general mental ability, or from independent multiple ones? With regard that this thing constitutes in itself an existing problem that psychologists encounter, which led to educational effects that reflect on learning and education in general.

Second: The question whether intelligence was inherited or acquired? In fact, answering these two questions had revealed what is intelligence and explained the psychology of thinking.

Attitudes of scientists differed in answering these questions. The following is an introduction to some theories that show the attitudes of psychologists toward intelligence:

1- Spearman Theory

Or the factors theory (general intelligence and specific intelligence):

Charles Spearman reached to his theory of intelligence through the use of factor analysis approach; he was the first one to introduce the statistical method in psychology.

Spearman reached to know the extent of overlapping or similarity between different mental tests, as well as their separation and independence from each other by establishing correlation factors between the results of these tests. He applied on a group of individuals several tests some of which are tests that measure features of mental activity and some are achievement tests. He reached as a result of this that each test made to measure mental activity contains one general common factor that exists in all mental tests and affects in every mental production. The test also contains a factor specific for each test. This factor is different from the specific factor in another test, so that whenever the saturation of the test in the general factor increases, specific factors are decreased in this test.

Spearman explains these results by saying:

All features of mental activity contain two factors, namely:

One general common factor, called G factor

One specific factor in every activity, called S factor

The general common factor in all features of mental activity is called "intelligence" or "general ability."

Accordingly, every mental outcome is affected by two factors, namely:

- One general factor, which affects this performance and every performance made by the individual.

- One specific factor, which its affect is limited to this performance only.

This means that various human abilities contain one general factor and its specific own factors. Whether in his ability in speech, logic thinking, political thinking, dealings, dealing with children, engineering design, drawing, home management, understanding literature …. etc. Therefore, this theory was called (The factors theory). Summary of the theory is a follows:

Intelligence is a general factor or general theoretical ability that affects in all types of mental activity but in different ratios, and participated with it in other factors that differ by mental processes. Therefore, individuals who have high proportions of intelligence are excellent in all aspects of mental activity despite of their difference in the degree of their excellence in various types of activities.

In addition, tests that measure the general mental ability is about realizing new relationships and concerns.

2-   Thorndike Theory

Or theory of (multiple factors-intelligence determined by neural network).

Thorndike believes that accurate analysis of intelligence shows that we must defined it psychologically. However, Thorndike submits a psychological definition by saying that intelligence is nothing but (abstract connection) or making connections. People vary in intelligence by their differences in number of connections of ideas of which their selves can make. He believes that intelligence is an outcome of a large number of connected mental abilities which is know now as (the multiple factors theory).

Thorndike goes to believe that intelligence in core depends on number and types of neural connections that the individual has. These connections connect between stimuli and respondents. Individual differences in intelligence are due to differences in neural connections suitable in individuals.

Thorndike built this opinion on researches conducted by him, where he applied (Cognitive) abilities tests that cognize (ability of abstract connection) on five hundred persons. Obtained results indicate that what is common between the (Cognitive) abilities was positively and largely compatible by (0.90) with what is common between other abilities which are (purely correlative) in the opinion of Thorndike who concludes by saying that compatibility of which his researches indicate cannot be truly explained unless if we assumed that the key element in intelligence is the ability of (abstract connection).

According to the data of this theory, Thorndike concludes the presence of three types of intelligence as follows:

a)   Mechanical or material intelligence. It is the ability of handling material subjects. It is apparent in motor and manual sensory skills.

b)   Abstract intelligence: Represents the ability to understand abstract symbols, ideas and meanings.

c)   Social intelligence: The ability of human to understand others.

3-   Thurstone Theory

Or theory of (primary factors-primary mental abilities).

Thurstone represents the trend of factor analysis in America. He published his researches in 1938 about the mental formation in which he concluded the determination of primary factors or mental primary abilities that he believes they share in formation of intelligence.

He applied several tests on a group of individuals. After analyzing the correlation factor matrix for the results of these tests, he concluded the determination of the following primary factors or primary mental abilities:

a)   Spatial ability: It appears in the individual ability in the perception of spatial relationships and different forms and be judged accurately, or in the perception of the situations of various things during movement.

b)   Numerical ability: It appears in the easiness of making main calculations: adding, multiplying, subtraction and division. This ability seems that it does not affected by cultural effects. This helps in explaining the existence of this ability in some individuals with an unusual appearance despite their failure in school achievement. Also, it helps in explaining its existence in the unlettered.

c)   Verbal ability: It appears in the individual ability in understanding the meanings of various vocabulary that reflect different ideas and meanings.

d)   Ability of verbal fluency: This ability refers to the verbal output that the individual uses in his speech and writings. This ability depends on letters and it appears in the individual who is fluent when using vocabulary.

e)   Ability of remembering: It appears in the individual ability in the direct remembering of a vocabulary combined with another, a number combined with another, or vocabulary combined with number.

f)   Ability of inductive reasoning: It appears in the individual ability in conclusion of the general base from parts.

g) Cognitive ability: It appears in speed and accuracy in realizing different details and parts.

Thurstone believes that each of the primary abilities is relatively independent from one another; this means that correlation between one ability tests is higher than the correlation between one ability tests and tests of other ability.

Thurstone objects on the presence of general factor or general mental ability as explained by (Spearman). He believes that intelligence is the outcome of mixture of these primary abilities with various ratios. This means that all abilities share in the formation of intelligence but in different ratios.

4-   Guilford Theory

Or (Intelligence is a three-dimensional complex structure):

Guilford tried to put a matrix that regulates the mental worlds. Therefore, he had developed a three-dimensional structure for the human brain. These dimensions came according to the following:

First: Processes:

This dimension contains five main mental abilities, as follows:

a)   Cognitive awareness: It is the ability that refers to all mental activities related to acquisition of knowledge.

b)   Memory: Refers to the ability of the individual in keeping what he acquires of knowledge and information and its methods of memorization and identification.

c)   Starting thinking: It is the ability that refers to ideal flexibility and ability to start thinking in several and multiple directions.

d)   Specific thinking: Refers to the ability of specifying the direction of thinking towards specific objective.

e)   Evaluation: Refers to mental activities that aim to verify the accuracy of available information and the extent of its validity in accomplishing certain task.

Second: Content:

This dimension represents the contents of the mind. It contains four types, as follows:

a)   Configurable content: Contains what can be perceived by senses such as size, image, location, pattern and voice … etc.

b)   Symbolic content: Refers to abstract shapes that symbolize certain symbols or things, such as letters, numbers, signals … etc.

c)   Moral or semantic content: Contains the meanings of vocabularies and ideas contained by these vocabularies. This level is basically appeared in language.

d)   Behavioral content: Refers to social content of which the motor behavior contains, such as actions, movements, gestures and expressive facial movements … etc.

Third: Outcomes

This dimension represents what resulted by interaction between processes and contents. The dimension contains six types of outcomes, as follows:

a) Unites, b) Categories, c) Relationships, d) Systems, e) Conversions and f) Inclusions.

These outcomes can be understood by their relationship with the dimensions of process and content. The mental process (remembering for example) addresses certain content (symbols for example), thus the result is (units) such as remembering names, letters or numbers, (categories) such as remembering static or animated characters, or (relationships) such as remembering the relationship between two symbols or more ….. and so on for the five mental processes and the four contents.

As a result of the interaction of the three-dimensional contents of the mind 5 × 4 ×6, 120 separated mental abilities are resulted.

After this introduction of Guilford form, it is possible to conclude the following:

- Guilford presents a valuable framework useful for the discovery and determination of multiple components of intelligence. He implies that some relatively-complex forms of learning, such as solving problems, require compiling between numbers of several abilities that must be available to do such type of learning.

- Guilford form approves the idea stating that the learner who acquires and store information and storage can use them as necessary.

- This form supports the idea of presence of various types of intelligence and helps in explaining the individual differences in terms of some abilities, where this form explains factors that lead to the excellence of some individuals in certain fields.

5- Vernon Theory

(Or the pyrmidical structure of intelligence):

Vernon says that components of intelligence are arranged pyrmidically. On the top of the pyramid lies a general factor that is positively connected with all other mental abilities, followed in terms of ranking in the pyrmidical organization two groups of main denominated factors. One of these factors represents the group of verbal-educational factors, beneath it a group of secondary dominated factors (or specific factors) such as creative thinking factors, verbal relationship and numerical ability factors … etc.

While the second main denominated factors represent the spatial-mechanic factors group, beneath it a group of secondary denominated factors, or specific factors, such as factors of spatial ability (Cognizance of dimension, location, size and shape … etc), factors of motor-psychological ability and mechanical knowledge factors … etc.

The pyrmidical organization of intelligence refers to the extent of the narrowness and wideness of the behavioral field connected to various levels for this organization. Level of mental abilities graded in the organization were higher, the more general and less specific the behavioral field connected to it and vice versa.

The idea of pyrmidical organization of intelligence's components is of vital educational importance, so as teachers are able to classify instructional objectives and tasks according to what is required by several cognitive abilities to achieve it.

6-   Cattell Theory:

(Or flexible intelligence and specific intelligence)

Cattell divides intelligence into two different types:
1-   Flexible (or fluid) intelligence.

2-   Specific (or crystallized) intelligence.

- Flexible (or Fluid) Intelligence:

Cattell focuses on this type of intelligence that basically indicates to non-verbal mental ability that is relatively free from the effects of cultural factors. For example the ability to classify shapes, and to cognize sequences (numerical, verbatim and formal), correlated matrixes and formal analyses.

Specific (or Crystallized) Intelligence:

This in turn indicates to knowledge and skills that are strongly affected by cultural factors, such as general information, vocabulary, abstract vocabulary measures or comparisons and all different vocabulary mechanisms.

Cattell believes that tests that measure ability of mathematical reasoning, ability of vocabulary inductive reasoning, and the ability of logic measure include both types of flexible and specific intelligence, as for the tests of (Stanford-Binet-) and (Wechsler.)

Flexible intelligence is more dependent on psychological structures that support the mental behavior. This type of intelligence increases-since birth until a certain age of adolescence, where this type starts after this inclination as a result of natural gradual dissolution of these psychological structures. It is also more sensitive and is liable to be affected by the brain harm cases of the specific intelligence.

While specific intelligence reflects the process of cultural assimilation. It is largely affected by formal or informal learning during different stages of life. However, specific intelligence does not developed except by practicing or using the pattern of flexible intelligence.

7- Jensen Theory

(Or correlated intelligence and cognitive intelligence)

Jensen classifies mental abilities into two categories as follows:
- Category of correlated abilities or level one.

- Category of cognitive abilities or level two.

The first category includes the memorized learning (memorization) and short term memory; it is measured by ability to remember numbers and free memorization, sequential learning and learning of correlated pairs.

While the second category includes the ability of reasoning and solving problems, it is usually measured by abilities that contain tests of general intelligence, especially those tests that contain deductive inductive reasoning, solving problems, using concepts, image measurement, numerical chains and consecutive matrices.

Difference takes shape between the two categories-according to Jensen's opinion-in the degree or level of complexion of conversion processes and mental treatments by which these abilities require. Correlated abilities require simple conversion processes for stimuli inputs, while cognitive abilities require more complex mental treatments and conversion processes.

8- Piaget Theory

(Or intelligence as a form of biological adaptation between individual and environment).

Intelligence in Piaget is a form of biological adaptation between the individual and the environmental. This adaptation exemplifies by attempting of the individual to keep a type of balance between his own needs and requirements imposed by the environment.

Piaget goes to believe that mental processes are not a direct function of learning nor they are direct function of biological growth, yet mental abilities are a function of the process of reorganizing cognitive structures resulted from organic-environmental interactions occurring through the cognitive development.

Piaget Theory takes in intelligence the form of pyrmidical form that contains four basic stages of mental development, each of which takes a form of cognitive organization. These stages represent forms of biological adaptation and occur sequentially as a result of the interaction of the individual with his environment. Occurring of any stage depends on the previous one, as well as it does not exceed the next stage.

Measurement of Intelligence and its Tests

Measurement of Intelligence, or General Mental Ability:

Mental measurement was affected by approaches of natural and psychological sciences. Scientists believed that intelligence is a natural force in human being, which can be measured by motor sensory processes because they believe that senses are the base of the mind. Measures and tests appeared which measure the motor sensory functions to infer the mental functions.

Sensory measurement means have developed until they become a measure of upper sensory functions such as visual discrimination between various geometric shapes, auditory discrimination between sounds and measurement of feedback time.

Researches have shown weak correlation between motor sensory aspects and intelligence. Therefore, scientists turn towards the study of intelligence by measuring the upper mental processes such as thinking, imagination and remembering.

Intelligence Measurement Unit

Difference between intelligent person and unintelligent one appears in the ability to solve problems and behave in new situations. Effect of intelligence appears in speed, creation, concentration of energy and overcome difficulties. Given the importance of intelligence factor, scientists singled out special measurement unit that measures the mental age of the person. Mental age of the person is the level that is corresponding to middle age in a specific stage compared to most of the individuals who are middle in that age. In comparison with the mental age with chronological age of the individual, we conclude the intelligence ratio.

The German scientist Stern has explained the importance of intelligence ratio in determining the extent of delay or progress of intelligence paths and levels. Therefore, he suggested dividing mental age on chronological age and multiplying the result in one hundred. The result of this process is called intelligence ratio, in other words:

$$\text{Intelligence ratio} = \frac{\text{Mental age}}{\text{Chronological age}} \times 100$$

Example: Find the intelligence ratio of three students, mental age of each one of them is 8 years, while the chronological age of the first student is 16, the second student 8 and the third student 5 years. By using the previous equation, we can calculate the intelligence ratios of the three students in the following way:

Intelligence ratio of the first student = $\frac{8}{6} \times 100 = 50$, this indicates mental retardation.

Intelligence ratio of the second student = $\frac{8}{8} \times 100 = 100$, this indicates normal intelligence

Intelligence ratio of the third student = $\frac{8}{5} \times 100 = 160$, this means geniality.

It is clear from the above that equality of the mental age with chronological age makes the intelligence ratio 100, while if the mental age is less than the chronological age, then the intelligence ratio is less the 100.

Distribution of Intelligence Grades (Strata of Intelligent):

Statistical researches and studies indicated that distribution in human beings is generally subject to usual pattern. When applying one of the intelligence tests on a random sample represented for specific statistical community, such as secondary school students in a community, and pure grades obtained by the subjects were converted to standard grades of (100) mediation and (16) standard deviation, we will find that majority in the middle of the curve are normal intelligent, where most of the grades are concentrated around mediation, then distribution graduates on both side until we find a minority of geniuses in one part, and minority of weak minded in another. Between these two parts we find graded strata of various intelligence levels, as shown in the following figure:

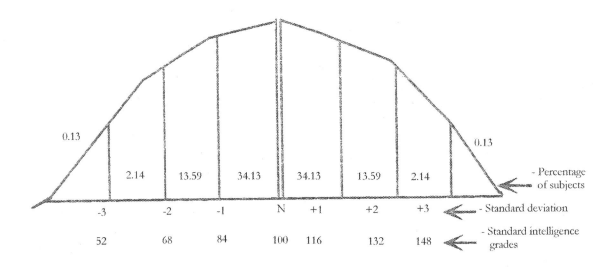

It is shown from this figure that grades of one-third of the statistical community's individuals were ranged between 84 and 116 grades while grades of the remaining one-sixth of community' individuals is less than 84 grades. Grades of the other one-sixth are more than 116 grades.

Most of intelligence tests were developed so as their standard grades are distributed the same way shown in the previous figure.

It is noted that distribution does not reach this degree of similarity except when number of individuals increases so as all strata represent the best representation. Whereas this is subject to the circumstances of researches and selection of samples, we rarely find full similarity in distribution in the different scientist's results. Besides, scientists differ in their selection of the limits of intelligence strata and various levels and the extent of the wideness and narrowness of these strata. This explains the difference among them in the percentage of number of individuals in any of the intelligence strata such as percentages of geniuses, middle-intelligent or mentally related.

Classification of Standard Grades of Intelligence:

Classification of standard grades of intelligence is made in seven categories. Each category has its own range of grades as shown in the following table:

A table shows the classification of standard grades in seven different categories of intelligence.

Categories of Intelligence	Standard Grades of Intelligence (Intelligence ratio)
1- Weak minded category	69 and less
2- Limit weak minded category	70-79
3- Below average category	80-89
4- Average category	90-109
5- Above average category	110-120
6- Intelligent category	121-130
7- Super intelligent category	131 and more

Intelligence and its Types:

Scientists tended to develop several tests that measure intelligence. It is possible to classify intelligence tests into the following:

First: vocabulary tests, include the following:
a) Individual vocabulary tests, b) Collective vocabulary tests

Second: Practical tests, include the following:
a) Individual practical tests, b) Collective practical tests

Third: Talents and abilities test

First) Vocabulary Tests:

These tests are composed of questions answered by the individual with verbal answers. Such tests deal with various aspects which answering discloses the processes of which intelligence include. These tests are made individually or collectively.

a) Individual vocabulary tests:

This type of tests measures the intelligence of individuals one by one. Therefore, these tests take long time until they are made on a group of individuals.

These tests are used in cases in which the study of the individual requires individual study in psychological clinics.

One of the examples of these tests is (Stanford-Binet) test, 1960, which is considered the most commonly used intelligent tests. This test contains twenty groups of tests that deal with individuals who are between two years of age and adulthood. Such test is divided according to certain intervals mainly composed of verbal questions regarding vocabulary, understanding and general information. These tests require vocabulary responses.

Also, one of the examples of these tests is (Wechsler) tests for children and adults. They are vocabulary and performance tests. Vocabulary tests deal with general information, understanding, mathematical reasoning, remembering, similarities and vocabulary. Performance tests deal with completing pictures, organizing shapes, cubes, collecting things and processing numerical symbols.

b) Collective vocabulary tests:

These tests measure the intelligence of many individuals at one time. Therefore these tests are used in selecting large numbers of individuals: in factories, schools and army.

These tests include instructions that explain the idea of testing and method of answering and give solved examples explain so, followed by training questions then test questions. The instructions determine the period necessary for making the test.

The first test of this type appeared during the First World War from the psychological studies department of the U.S. Army, under which soldiers had been distributed on different troops, as well as weak-minded were eliminated from fighting.

This test is composed of two tests:
First: Vocabulary test suitable for measuring the intelligence of learned individuals. It is called Alpha test.

Second: Practical test suitable for measuring the intelligence of the unlettered and foreigners. It is called Beta test.

One of the examples of these collective vocabulary tests is the secondary intelligence test developed by Miss Mira in the Institute of Vocational Guidance in Barcelona. This test was adjusted by Professor Ismail Al-Qabbani. This test is suitable for measuring the intelligence of secondary schools students who are between twelve and eighteen years old.

This test is composed of small manual that contains fifty eight questions graduated in difficulty and preceded by instructions that explain the idea of the test. These instructions show the method of answering questions. Four solved questions are given as well as a period of forty minutes is specified for making the test.

Second: Practical tests:

These tests are made on knowing the general mental ability of the individual by his practical behavior.

This type of test is composed of mazes, pictures, drawings and geometric shapes… to which the individual respond by moving in corridors of the maze and escaping from the nearest way, by building a shape from a group of cubes, or making a picture from its scattered parts. These tests are suitable for measuring the intelligence of deaf and dumb, individuals with impaired speech, weak-minded, young children, unlettered and foreigners. Such tests are usually used in measuring the intelligence of unlettered workers and soldiers in order to direct them towards the work suitable for them. These tests are made individually or collectively.

a) Individual practical tests:
These tests are made individually. One of which is the mazes test for Porteus and test of panel forms and completing pictures of Seguin.

b) Collective practical tests:
These tests are made collectively. One of which is the pictorial intelligence test for children, sequential matrices test and foot drawing test.

Third: Readiness and Abilities Tests:

They are tests standardized on some basic abilities such as language ability, vocabulary ability, ability of abstract reasoning, and ability of solving problems. They are also rated on readiness of students to achieve in a certain school subject. As these tests deal with different aspects of the readiness of the learner to achieve in the vocabulary, mathematical, geometrical and technical fields …etc.

It should be noted that abilities measured by intelligence tests are more general and comprehensive than the abilities measured by the readiness tests. However, no test substitute the other, because intelligence tests measure a general readiness to learn, while readiness tests measure a specific readiness to learn in a narrow and specific range.

Intelligence Determinants

Subject of intelligence is one of the subjects where debate has rage about each of the impact of the environment and hereditary as factors that play an important role in determining the nature of intelligence.

Hereditary supporters had attributed the difference of intelligence between individuals to what the individual inherited from his parents through genes, while other party confirms the environmental aspect and believes that intelligence is resulted from the interaction of all external factors affecting the individual since the beginning of his creation until death. Each party submits several experiments by which he will prove his point of view.

In fact, this disagreement has a major importance and responsibility under which concepts and philosophies are determined. Such concepts and philosophies have social, economic and political results. When characteristics and traits are attributed to genetic origin, this includes the inevitability of surrender. Environment and education cannot be more than direction, while the person who denies the existence of inherited mental characteristics, he insists on the importance of education and factors of the environment in determining the fate of individuals and the human civilization.

In the midst of this discrepancy between supporters of hereditary and supporters of environment in determining intelligence, controversy increases with the emergence of the opinions of the scientist Jensen who presented his opinions in a scientific article mentioned and discussed by Dr. Abdul Majeed Nashwati in his book (The Educational Psychology), which we quoted here to enrich the presented subject and in conformation of the extent of importance of opinions presented in this article and in its discussion.

Jensen wonders in his article about the extent of ability of increasing the level of intelligence degrees and achievement of a certain groups of children.

Jensen starts his article with a presentation of evaluation results of the compensatory programs planned to help the children of disadvantaged and culturally disadvantages groups, showing its failure and ineffectiveness in increasing the level of these children mentally and educationally. He criticizes the main idea that lines these programs, which states that difference in intelligence grades is attributed primarily to environmental factors. He indicates through data discussed by him that 80% of these differences are attributed to genetic factors, while the environmental factors do not contribute in more than 20% in its events.

Jensen indicates that extreme environmental deprivation may prevent the achievement of children from their total genetic abilities. However, an educational program enriched with stimuli does not necessarily pay these children out the scope of their genetically-determined potentials.

On other hand, Jensen emphasizes on the presence of certain types of genetically-determined educational abilities. Such abilities appear as certain ethnic characteristics that characterize certain groups regardless of the economics, social or cultural factors. From which Jensen concludes an attitude stating that intelligence is a natural trait that constitutes one of the genetic factors distributed between individuals differently, and that intelligent and unintelligent can be anywhere within the individuals of any group regardless of race, environment and social class.

Jensen acknowledges expressly in his article of the insufficiency and uncertainty of human knowledge, on the level of genetic research, of reasons of genetic differences. He states that all researches discussed by him by review and discussion do not suggest any conclusive and direct evidence on the reasons of genetic differences, whether among individuals or among groups.

In the context of discussion of these opinions of the scientist Jensen, Dr. Nashwati believes that they are opinions that reflect a pessimistic image that ruins optimism by educational compensatory or remedial programs.

Dr. Nashwati comments on such by citing opinions critic for the image presented by Jensen, which are not free from arguments in opposition .Voyat shows by mistake the strategy followed by Jensen in determining the role of genetic and environmental factors in intelligence, which totally depend on statistical processors or on determination of honesty according to quantitative estimations only.

In addition, scientist Kagan, who in turn analyzed the same data from which Jensen derived his results, published these data in a way that confirms the importance of environmental factors more than genetic factors in determining grades of intelligence.

It is shown from what we presented that there is an obvious difference between genetic trend supporters and environmental trend supporters regarding the determination of the concept and nature of intelligence. There is nothing wrong in presenting forms of studies that discussed the relationship of these factors in opposition, aiming to determine the objective attitude from the hereditary and environment issue, which agree with the objective facts.

Intelligence and Hereditary:

Psychological studies indicate that intelligence is readiness inherited in the individual from his parents and ancestors. Therefore, intelligence trait accompanies the person throughout his life and is considered relatively-constant characteristics in the individual's personality. This does not mean that environment does not affect intelligence, instead the environment has its effect that appears in how to use the amount inherited from intelligence, in other words environment cannot increase the amount of the inherited intelligent, yet it can help in making use of the amount existed from intelligence.

The following are the most important evidences that prove intelligence is an inherited readiness:

1- Golton proved that children of intelligent and geniuses are usually intelligent. He made a study on relatives of great men in England who were judges, politicians, prime ministers and prominent leaders of literature, science, photography and music and others. He concluded from his research that great men usually have great relatives from among parents, ancestors, sons, grandsons or uncles, or alike.

2- Terman made a study on more than one thousand gifted children. He compared his studies with the same one made on ungifted children. He concluded results that support the result of Golton.

3- Some studies have shown that the more blood relationship strengthens the more similarity in intelligence increases. Therefore, we find that correlation factor between the intelligence of twins is 0.9, between brothers is 0.6 and between cousins is 0.35, while the correlation factor between those who are not related to family relationship is zero.

4- Some studies have shown that children who grow up since birth in one environment, such as abandoned children, do not look alike in intelligence, yet we find among them individual differences in intelligence. This is a testimony to the impact of genetic factor in intelligence.

5- Experiments have shown that improving the environment of weak-minded and unintelligent does not change their intelligence ratio and whatever we increase the level of environment we can not make the unintelligent intelligent or make the weak-minded genius.

Intelligence and Environment:

Supporters of the environment believe that human intelligence and abilities are determined by various factors of environment and there is no such impact for genetic factors. One of the leaders in this trend is Watson who says in his famous saying: (Give me a dozen healthy infants, well-formed, and my own specified world to bring them up in and I'll guarantee to take any one at random and train him to become any type of specialist I might select-doctor, lawyer, artist, merchant-chief and, yes, even beggar-man and thief, regardless of his talents, penchants, tendencies, abilities, vocations, and race of his ancestors.)

Supporters of such trend present models for savage children lived in different animal species and they earned its characteristics. The supporters take from these examples evidence on the role of the environment and its impact in the human growth.

One of these cases is the savage child found by hunters in Aviron forest in France in 1799. Etard the physician tried to train him to bring him back to human life. He eventually was able to do different daily activities but he could not reach the level of normal human being.

Also, the case of (wolf children): They are children found in the wolf caves in the forests of northern-western countries in India, they live like wolves. One of those children the child known is Sinikar. He was found by Indians living in a cave with wolves, so they carried him into one of the shelters. He was able after long training to walk on his feet and do simple things under supervision and observation.

Some researches and studies have shown that discouraging environment, which does not supply its children during their upbringing with appropriate stimulus in the field of some mental skills or abilities of which intelligence tests include; such environment retards the development of intelligence of those children. This also reflected by their performance on these tests. These evidences also indicate that the grade of this retardation is positively connected with the length of period of time that the children spent in the deprived or poor environment in terms of stimulus, and with growth stage that he is in during his exposure to such environment.

On the other hand, we find that the American geneticist Cattsman believes that differences existing in intelligence averages between black and white Americans are probably due in its sources to the impacts of environmental damages suffered by blacks through the stages of their lives.

Conclusion: The general mental ability of the individual is the result of continuous reaction between different genetic and environmental factors that work together since the first moment of the creation of the fetus. Cell proliferation is not made except within special circumstances that surrounds it. The reaction continues but it becomes more complex after birth due to the complexity of environmental factors surrounding the organism, especially social ones.

Here we must emphasize that inheritance of the individual of general mental ability is the inheritance of unlimited possibility that lead to different levels as a result to the reaction with various circumstances. Moreover, intelligence as a innate ability, supporters of hereditary were not able to discover it by means of measurement because it depends on the environmental and its experiences.

Using Intelligence Measures in Schools

Some U.S. states had stopped the processes of conducting collective tests in schools. The reason behind this is mishandling of some teachers with grades of intelligence of their students. These teachers are based on degrees of intelligence in the prediction of levels of achievement of students who were classified according to this base, without taking into consideration the matter of improving the educational conditions based on the environmental factors that affect in increasing such levels.

The teacher duty is to be aware of the impossibility of full integration of correlation between achievement and the grade of intelligence. This is due to the presence of other factors and stimuli that have its emphasizing role in the process of determining the levels of academic achievement of the learner. Even if intelligence indicates the extent of potentials of the individual, it does not predict whether this individual will achieve these potentials or not.

Grades of intelligence are considered as one of the several factors that affect the entity of human individual. Some of these factors are tendencies, trends, motives, values, interests and self-concept. Each of these factors has its direct effect on the mental ability

Unit Four

Cognitive Development

Content:

- Basic Concepts of Development, its Variables and Methods of Studying

- Principles of Development

- Stage and Critical Stage Concept

- Piaget Theory of Cognitive Development

- Bruner Theory of Cognitive Development

- Erikson Theory of Social Psychological Development

Cognitive Development

Basic Concepts of Development, its Variables and Methods of Studying

Meaning of Development:

Psychologists define development as the series of interrelated changes that occur in human being starting from conception to old age then senescence.

Development is both organic and functional at the same time. It is identified in two meanings: the first is the outward meaning represented in the changes that occur to the human body with regard to weight, length and size.

The second meaning is the deep meaning represented in the changes that occur to language, pronunciation and skills, in addition to intellectual, emotional and social changes and what these changes include of psychological and chemical changes.

It is concluded from this that development is a successive series of changes the former of which affects the later accompanied by the disappearance in the human qualities and the appearance of other qualities according to a dynamics that persistently seeks to carrying on the human life circle.

In the framework of this meaning of development and its variables, it could be said that development process includes two concepts which are increase and change.

The increase means the quantitative accumulations that lead to the increase in weight, size and cells number, while change refers to the qualitative differences that occur to the organism. From this starting point, growth can be considered as a process in which bodily and physiological changes are completed with the psychological changes to improve the individual ability to control his environment. Completeness here indicates the organic attachment of the bodily, intellectual, emotional and social changes…. this completed development aims at the end at the individual mastering a set of tasks that are different from age to age, to enable him to control environment and adapt with and for it in a positive way to achieve his well-being and happiness.

Methods of studying development

Specialists in development psychology were keen to choose the suitable methods and the most effective means to examine questions about the subject of their study concerning human growth. Of the most prominent methods used in this domain are the following:

First: Correlational methods

These methods are used when raising a question such as what is correlated to what? For example, if we wanted to know the manner of increase in the linguistic words for a child between three and six years, we ask correlational question, meaning we want to stand on the number of vocabulary related to a certain age. To answer this question we resort to one of these correlational methods. Of the most prominent means used in these methods what follows:

1- Observation.   2- Case study.   3- Interview.

Second: Causation (experimental) methods

When the researcher interest is directed to the causation relationships between the phenomena he is studying, he usually resorts to experiment which is of the most important methods that involve achieving components of the scientific methodology. Experimental trend in psychology indicates the most problems of psychology if not the whole of its problems, may be studied through field experiment in the laboratory or in experimental sites.

Of the most prominent methods there are laboratory experimentation and natural experimentation.

Third: Differentiation methods

Psychologist usually resorts to one of the differentiation methods when his interest centers on working with the child as an individual person, not with a group of children, where he uses psychological and intellectual tests (intelligence tests), projective tests, self report methods and playing observations.

In the framework of using these differentiation methods, the researcher always compares with a standard group, whether implicitly or explicitly, so as to be able to determine the extent to which the individual is similar or different from the used standard. An important problem focuses on the using of differentiation methods in making sure of the extent of the appropriateness of the standard group that we compare or compare it with a certain child.

Fourth: Follow-up methods

These methods focus on observing the human growth in its different bodily, intellectual, emotional and social dimensions along successive periods of age that start from the beginning of life, and then proceed in its consecutive stages, by registering all what associated with that dimension including aspects, behavior and emotion. Follow-up methods have two trends, namely:

Longitudinal trend or longitudinal method:

In this trend the researcher continues his follow-up of cohort of individuals throughout a period of time that may exceed ten years in some cases, where he studies throughout this period a separate subject according to systematic periodical periods. Thus, this method provides us with information about models and process of change on the long-term. Such method provides exact information; however, it is expensive and requires effort, time and money.

Cross-sectional trend or cross-sectional method:

The researcher in this method focuses on one of the growth dimensions, bodily, mentally or emotionally in a group of individuals from one age. In general, this method is much easier than the longitudinal method regarding saving time and effort.

However, in the combination of the longitudinal method and cross-sectional method, the researcher can avoid many problems that might face both methods. In their integration the researcher can study individuals of different formation dimensions in consecutive years of growth. Also, each method provides the other with facts related to identifying research and analysis places. This combination between these two methods, the longitudinal and cross-sectional, is what is called normative studies.

Principles of Development

Development process is based on principles and laws that determine the nature of its course and progress. It is possible to outline these principles in what follows:

1- The existence of correlation between growth aspects. This becomes clear when we find that intellectual development and emotional development are greatly affected by the social development or the bodily development. A defect in height or excess obesity may make the child undergo states of shame and isolation. Motor development is also connected to nervous development and intellectual development is connected to linguistic and motor development. This means that different aspects of development work together in conformity and harmony.

2- The difference of development is in its pace rate between one stage and other age stages. Development here goes according to a continuation system in spite of the difference in its pace that is characterized by instability in all stages of age. Growth rate is different from one child to another, but the sequence of development is unified for all children.

3- Development process is characterized by being a successive process. Standing for the child precedes walking, sitting precedes standing, walking precedes running….. It is observed that the child talks tenderly before talking. He pronounces the word that takes the place of a sentence before he attaches words in useful sentences.

4- Every part of the body has a growth course related to it. The nervous curve related to the development of the nervous system, which includes development direction for the head, nerves, spinal cord and the eye is characterized by fast development in early childhood and before long it turns into slower development during early childhood and adolescence stage.

5- Development goes from the general and outlined to the private, distinct and detailed. The child starts from the full rushing of the body towards objects to stretching his hand towards them. He then shifts to grapping objects with part of the hand, i.e. with finger tips. For example, he starts writing by drawing meaningless lines, then he shifts to writing letters a , b or c. He also becomes fluent in his language by saying papa to any man. He then assigns it only to his father when calling him.

6- Every person is characterized by a pace in growth pertaining to him. The individual grows in a pace different from the growth of others, which clearly and plainly manifests the difference existing between individuals.

7- Development occurs according to a specific pattern where it is directed from top to bottom, i.e. from head to legs, from the center to the edges. This principle refers to an obvious pattern in body development especially in stages of fetus creation. However, it is also true in terms of the development of social relationships that advance from egocentrism to the expansion of the social relationships framework of the individual.

8- All children usually pass through the same different growth stages according to the sequence in which these stages appear.

9- Development and learning overlap with the individual behavior in a way that becomes difficult to put separating borders between changes resulting from maturity and changes resulting from learning.

10- The human being grows internally. His growth either comes through cells division, so number of these cells increases, or through the increase in weight or size of these cells. The human being in his structure is different from the building that is heightened floor above floor by adding to brick after brick.

11- Development progresses from general to private. Behavior starts from the general overall activity to more concentrated and specified responses. Also, the effective motor control is practiced first on the basic muscles that raise the head, then comes later controlling muscles of arms and shoulders, afterwards muscles of legs are controlled.

Stage in Development Concept

Stages concept constitutes an important and basic dimension in the subject of human development. In this issue, a broad question emerges that says: Is it true that the child's development passes through specific time stages as indicated by some development psychologists?

Answering this question is not an easy matter, considering that stages concept is still surrounded by mystery in psychology, and the difference in opinions and theories is still existing concerning whether development is still continuous, meaning it is progressing gradually without any severe or sudden changes .

Human development in points of views of researchers in psychology contains characteristics of continuity and non continuity in terms that human development passes through continuous development and according to specific stages, so that the characteristics of continuous development and characteristics of stage development synchronize. Though the human being passes through different stages in which considerable changes happen on his behavior patterns, he maintains his general form and identity during his growth process.

Researchers resort to using the stage concept in development psychology as an indication of the changes that happen to behavior patterns during different development stages. Accordingly, the stage meaning is what refers to a group of behavior patterns that are associated together during its occurrence, so as such patterns can be classified logically. For example, the behavior patterns related to early or late childhood stage, adolescence stage or other stages. A number of psychologists used the stage concept in describing some aspects of development such as the psychological, moral or cognitive development.

Critical Stage in Development Concept

Development psychologists indicate that there are crucial periods of great sensitivity in the development of children through which learning behavioral patterns becomes possible. On other hand, they indicate that there must be certain environmental interactions available during this critical period in order for the development to progress normally. The conclusive factor here is timing. If a suitable interaction didn't occur during a specific period, we find that development might go slowly and stop. In another meaning, there are convenient periods and others inconvenient in the development of learning certain skills. Children who receive praise and tribute for their early linguistic attempts are more tended to speak fluently in an early age, compared to children who do not receive verbal stimulation when they are willing and ready to learn. On the whole, the child who lacks the opportunity of learning is expected to face difficulties in the development of other learned responses that would be helpful for school learning.

The concept of critical or crucial periods was widely used by researchers in the social and emotional development as well as the cognitive development. Perhaps the concept of the critical period is one of the important concepts that must be taken into account when studying human development, because it involves implications relevant to the educational process. Providing the child with the suitable stimuli in the different development periods, whether these periods were critical or not, helps the child achieving a normal development, that development that is considered one of the most important aims education is looking for.

"Piaget's Theory of Cognitive Development"

- Approaches of cognitive development.

- The basic cognitive processes.

- Piaget's stages in cognitive development and its applications in the class.

- The application of Piaget's theory in education.

Approaches of cognitive development

The study of "thinking development in the human being" or "how the human being learn to think" has a notable and important position in the context and subjects of psychology, especially educational psychology.

Interest in this study is aimed at the issue of cognitive development represented in thinking types prevailing in each of the successive growth stages and the changes that occur on these stages.

The study of the cognitive development readiness or the development of the thinking ability, from Jean-Piaget point of view, forms the first components of tribal behavior. The theory being created by this domain is considered one of the most common theories of cognitive development in psychology domains, and one of the most influential in the cognitive (intellectual) curve of learning. Given the importance of such theory, we must know (Piaget's) point of view in the matter of psychological development and know the basic terms and concepts raised by him. Then we research the cognitive development stages that he was interested in, since his interest focused on the intellectual and cognitive development that happens to the normal person through transformation from stage of infant who produces unrelated overt and primitive reflexive actions until maturity stage that is characterized by skillful actions. His theory gave some answers to the questions raised by those interested in psychology of thinking about the origin of the compound behavior.

Piaget's basic cognitive processes:

Piaget believes that there are two main functions of thinking that do not change with age and they are: (organization) and (adaptation). These functions are considered two innate characteristics that lead the overall behavioral development of the human being. Thereby everything the human being knows and can do, want to do and actually do it in each of his development stages tends to be highly organized and integral.

Organization denotes the resultant cognitive construction to the individual. It consists of correlated integrated cognitive units. The function of organization exemplifies in the individual tendency to organize and coordinate intellectual processes in overall coordinated and integrated systems. Function of adaptation exemplifies in the individual tendency to adapt and harmonize with the environment he lives in. In spite that this function is general for all people, yet every individual has a special way in adapting with the environment. Adaptation is the constructional or functional expression that achieves for the human organism his survival. Thus Piaget strongly relates between psychological and biological processes.

These two functions of organization and adaptation as we know are basic for the organism for the continuation of its survival. The human being cannot survive unless he organizes the biological processes in a way that brings coordination and integration between them. He also cannot survive if he was not able to adapt with the environment he lives in. Piaget indeed grants these two characteristics to the human cognitive thought.

Piaget looks at adaptation on the basis of two integrated processes, namely: assimilation and accommodation.

Assimilation is the individual tendency to give greater weight to things from the external world in his mental construction or the structure he has as if the individual changes the image of a thing so as to suite what he knows.

While accommodation is the individual's tendency to change his response so as to accommodate with the surrounding environment as if the individual changes his mental structures to face the environment demands that is to change what is in himself so as to accommodate the new stimulus that he is exposed to as if to give it a meaning of what is available of meanings at hand. Perhaps the following example illustrates what is meant: the mother has already taught her child the word bird, and to say a bird when he sees the bird flying. One day while the child was going on a picnic in the park with his mother he saw a butterfly flying around him so he said to his mother: "Look this is a bird." He thereby assimilated the butterfly, i.e. he changed its characteristics so as to fit the image he got. This image is the image that implies to him that everything that flies is a bird. But when his mother says: "This is a butterfly not a bird", a meaning will be generated to him saying: "not everything that flies is a bird", i.e. he begins to change the internal meaning so as to fit the new stimuli he is exposed to. If he says next time butterfly when he sees the butterfly he is giving an evidence of accommodation.

The previous example manifests that assimilation and accommodation are two integral processes and that achieving equilibration between them is necessary for the new adaptation and for the development of the child's intelligence.

As we have seen, the new experience is the one that prompted the child to assimilate new objects then accommodate and adapt with it. However, exposing the child to experience much more of his ability to accommodate, might be harmful. From here importance of Piaget's idea of equilibration emerges in the development of intelligence. He looks to intelligence as a kind of equilibration that all mental structures seek to, i.e. to achieve the coordinated equilibrium between mental processes and the circumstances surrounding the human being.

Piaget attributes the mental development process in children to the continuous activity of assimilation and accommodation as the organism is in a state of intelligent agreement when the two processes of assimilation and accommodation balance. When these two processes are unbalanced state, accommodation becomes active at the expense of assimilation which leads to imitation and mimicry. Assimilation, which helps to create agreement and harmony between the new learning experiences in the range of the organism's need, will prevail in the state of balanced work of the two processes.

Thus, mental or cognitive development in Piaget's point of view is a kind of sequence of disequilibrium and regaining equilibrium during interaction with the environment. This is by using assimilation and accommodation in an integrated manner. Transition from one mental growth stage to the next occurs in a gradual, developing way, organized in a pyramidical system of which the sensorimotor stage forms its base and the abstract intellectual processes forms its peak.

Thus, the individual realizes the environment from the mental structures he has. Disequilibrium occurs in the individual when his mental structures do not help him in realizing it clearly which leads to accommodation that produces change and development in the prevailing mental structures to enable the individual to realize the environment and its new elements. This is done by gaining and learning new mental structures or strategies that help the organism to regain equilibrium.

The organism maintains this equilibrium until he faces other new situations so he again assimilates his equilibrium and works again to regain his balance.... Thus he learns, acquires and advances from one growth stage to the following stage.

Piaget's factors of cognitive development:

Piaget identifies factors that define learning and development average in the range of the cognitive development stages. He identifies these factors in four factors, which are:

1- **Maturity**: Environmental factors affect the cognitive development of the child only when the child is ready, that is biologically mature.

2- **Activity**: Cognitive development occurs through the active interaction between the child and the environment with what fits his biological maturity, and in the amount that interaction has meaning for the child.

3- **Environment**: Cognitive development occurs when the environment provides the child the cognitive stimuli and information through interaction and experience.

4- **Equilibrium**: Cognitive development occurs in learning when the child faces a situation that leads to disequilibrium in the child between what he got of abilities and strategies and what the opposite situation requires, which force the child to develop what he got and rearrange the situation with what fits with the new elements.

In the framework of what has been reviewed by Piaget's cognitive theory, it is possible to conclude the following principles:

a) Intelligence is the ability to transform information received from the environment, this ability and processes that include in such ability changes with the change of age.

b) Cognitive development occurs from stages of processes to a new stage through interaction and experience.

c) Development is a relationship between experience and maturity.

    d) Moderate challenge, disequilibrium and regaining equilibrium all are considered developing teaching processes.

Piaget's stages in cognitive development and its applications in the class:

Piaget divides mental development stages on which he built his theory in learning into four distinct stages, namely:

1- Sensorimotor stage: form birth until two years.

2- Preoperational stage: from 2 until 7 years.

3- Concrete operational state: from 7 until 11 years.

4- Formal operational stage: from 11 years.

The following is simple details about each of these stages as was mentioned by both Dr. Mohyi Eddinen Touq and Dr. Abdul Rahman Adas, which help in understanding and comprehend it.

1- Sensorimotor stage

This stage extends from birth to the end of the second year of age. In this stage-according to Piaget's opinion-beginnings of all intellectual structures or constructions form, partially or wholly. These structures are those that will enable the child to develop his intelligence later on.

Despite that the child lacks the ability to deal with symbols in the beginning of this stage; he turns from a weak and negative creature to an active one who is capable of some talking and good social adaptation.

Piaget looks at the interaction resulting between the motor activity and perception as the basis in children's thinking in the first and second years. Therefore, he calls this stage the sensorimotor thinking.

In this stage, the child is preoccupied in discovering the relationship between sensations and motor behavior. He is learning to what distance he must stretch out his hand to grip an object, what happens when he push the food dish from the table. He also learns that his hand is a part of him while the bed pillar is not. Through a large number of experiments, the child learns to distinguish between him and the external reality.

The most important discoveries in this stage are the concept of object-permanency-in other words to understand that object continues to exist even when it is not present now. If we covered the toy of the little child who is eight months old with a cloth piece at the time he was stretching his hand towards it, he stops stretching his hand and seems careless.

At the same time, he doesn't seem upset or surprised and acts as if the toy wasn't there, compared to the tenth month child who will actively look for the object that was hidden from him. He acts as if he is aware that the object is still there, despite that his searching is limited. If a child was used to find his toy in a specific place, he will go and look there first, in spite that he saw the toy being hidden in another place. He doesn't look for the toy in the last place he saw except at the end of the second year.

This stage is divided into six sub intervals, stages or phases, which are the following:
a) First sub-stage: It extends from birth to the end of the first month of age. In this phase the child practices reflexes that were born with him. As a result of practice his learning of these reflexes will improve and through such it he interacts with others who provide him with experiences. The most important reflexes in this sub-stage are actions of sucking, waving with hands and legs, nursing and excretion…etc.

b) Second sub-stage: It extends from the beginning of the second month to the end of the fourth month. In this phase the child coordinates between his reflexes and his responses, where the hands moves become consistent with the eyes, as the child pays attention to the sound source. He also succeeds in reaching grasping and sucking objects.

c) Third sub-stage: It extends from the beginning of the fifth month to the end of the eighth month. The child starts in this phase to expect the results of things including his actions. He can intentionally repeat the responses that led to important results for him. He also starts to pay attention to objects from the external world, where he starts looking for something he saw then disappeared.

d) Forth sub-stage: It extends from the beginning of the ninth month to the end of the thirteenth month. In this phase the child distinguishes between means and ends and starts to use suitable means to reach his ends. He is looking for his toy that he hides by useful means.

e) Fifth sub-stage: It extends from the beginning of the fourteenth month to the end of eighteenth month. In this phase the child resorts to experiment, discovery, adjustment and change with his behavior. He drops objects so as to see them falling, and he pushes things around him by a stick in his hand.

f) Sixth sub-stage: It extends from the end of the eighteenth month to the end of the second year of age. In this phase response to objects and events that the child observes in front of him starts, he also starts to think of them. He also invents new means to meet certain goals, all that is through his fantasies and thoughts. He for example pulls something towards him with a stick despite that he absolutely didn't use that before.

In short, this stage ends by the emergence of a simple degree of remembering, planning, imagination and pretending, which clears the way for the most complicated patterns of thinking as we will see.

2- Preoperational stage

This stage extends from the second year to the seventh year. It is characterized by the appearance of symbolic functions and language as a mean to represent environmental stimuli. Instead of the child being responsive to the physical stimuli in the environment, he forms in this stage symbols to represent these objects. He can also recreate or imitate some actions that occurred in front of him before hours.

The child's earlier interaction with the environment was direct and immediate, while he is able in this stage to represent objects intellectually and storing them for using later, yet he cannot solve a number of problems that seem intuitive for adults such as changing quantities when putting them in different tubes. This stage is divided into two phases:

a) The phase pre-concepts from 2 to 4 years. In this phase the child can perform simple classification operations, according to one aspect such as a size for example. Also, the obvious contradictions do not annoy the child (the relationship between weight and size, a big and light object was floating and a small and heavy object was sinking).

b) The intuitive phase from 4 to 7 years. The child in this phase makes some more difficult classifications, intuitively, that is without a rule that he knows. He also doesn't pay a clear attention to what he is doing. In this stage the gradual awareness starts by permanency of the characteristics. Piaget used experiments related to the phenomenon of permanency or conservation in studying intellectual processes of the child in the preoperational stage. As for us we adults, conservation principles seem extremely natural and normal. Therefore, quantity (mass) of something does not change when its shape changes or when divided into parts.

A child who is less than seven years does not realize concepts of memorization except with difficulty, because his thinking is still dominated by visual impressions. Change in perceptual characteristics is more important than the basic ones, such as the paste volume or the liquid quantity. The child's dependency on the visual impressions becomes more obvious if we look at the following experiment:

Six cups of coffee in front of the child are placed, and opposite to them six saucers for these cups. The child is asked to count the saucers and the cups and decide the equality between saucers and cups. Then saucers are placed above each other and the child is asked to decide whether the saucers number was equal to cups number, or that one of them is more than the other. The child says that the cups number is more than the saucers numbers. On other hand, the seventh year child assumes that the number of equal objects before still equals later. As for him the numerical equality is more important than the visual impressions.

3- Material-factual thinking stage

This stage extends from the end of the seventh year to the end of eleventh year. The child is able during this stage to solve the problem of quantities permanency. Also, the child in this stage starts to sort between classifications of living and solid objects. He can coordinate between the process of verbal counting and identifying numbers by using specific materials. Thus, he gives the evidence to use this process as a functional tool. He also can solve some problems through litigations instead of trial and error fashion. He also can distinguish between the present and past time.

However, the child can't perform some processes characterized by certain linguistic representations, such as the question "Is your dad a father or a man?" This is in spite that all these concepts are available separately to the child.

The child in this stage is unable to form abstract processes and concepts, like developing theories and comprehending abstract words, in spite of his understanding of some of the relationships between different things in the environment. He cannot imagine abstractly things that don't have reality such as the phenomenon of objects flotation. The child can reach a rule that says that heavy objects sink, but the changes in this law will confuse him like a big wooden piece doesn't sink.

In this stage, external actions alter to internal actions. Of progress aspects in the child's thinking in this stage are the following:

a) The development of his ability to sort.

b)   The child slowly progresses in shaping the concept of time.

c)   The child's ability to use concepts of Euclidean geometry.

In spite of the progress in the child's thinking in this stage, compared to the previous ones, yet he suffers some difficulties that hinder sound reasoning. Of these difficulties what follows:

- Weakness of his ability to verbal reasoning.

- Weakness of his ability to discover the logical fallacies.

- His failure in front of assignments that contradict reality.

4- Abstract thinking stage

This stage extends from 12 to 15 years. However, using this kind of thinking continues to the end of life.

This stage is characterized with the previous stage (concrete operational stage) by the appearance of processes as a characteristic distinguished by what preceded of stages. However, this does not mean that this stage represents the peak of the previous stages, instead it is a stage in which a new structure appears or this stage leads to a high level of equilibrium. The difference between who is five and who is fifteen years of age is not quantitative difference only, but it is a qualitative difference also.

Equilibrium in this stage is characterized by four important social characteristics that describe the highly self organization of human thought, namely:

a) The social world becomes united and of laws, organizations, rules, divisions and jobs.

b) Egocentrism is eliminated and the individual advances towards feeling of social perfection.

c)   Personality development depends on changing beliefs through self communication.

d)   Meaning of equality replaces undergoing the adults' behavior.

These characteristics form the basics of moral and social growth of the individual in this stage of age.

The most important characteristic of this stage is that the individual can solve problems that require hypothetical thinking-reasoning that is based on knowing all the following organizations:

a) Simple classification for a stable criterion.

b) Passing from classification to causation relationships and vice versa.

c) Sorting on the base of several criteria.

d) Expecting sorting results.

e) Passing successfully from sorting to relative law, and going back to another sorting then to a law and so on. This is called (reversibility).

f) Ambiguity in experimentation.

These organizations are from the previous-concrete-stage accomplishments. The most important concepts that became available for the individual in this stage are concepts of proportions and proportionality, equilibrium, possibility concepts, laws induction and factors analysis. This stage is generally characterized by the following:

1- The individual knows at the beginning of this stage that ways and means in the previous stage do not lead to a complete or comprehensive understanding of his problems, so his dependence on handling concrete objects becomes little.

2- The two processes of assimilation and accommodation are balanced in this stage.

3- Presence of deductive hypothetical reasoning in second degree relations-abstract relations-is considered a main criterion to prove reaching this final shape of thinking.

4- The individual develops the ability to imagine possibilities included in a situation formed before he provides the practical solutions of this situation.

5- The individual thinks beyond present and develops theories about everything, or thus thinking focuses on relationships not on the content. The individual thought held on to what is possible in an equal way to his holding on the reality, even his dependence on concrete facts and objects becomes little. He starts to use abstract issues more than using pure reality. The adolescent is no longer satisfied with events as it happen, but he considers them evidences to what he deems possible. He draws conclusions from issues he does not accept as fact, yet he examines its results then he later decides whether it was really true or not.

6- The individual's ability to think scientifically and to think as a scientist appears.

7- The ability to deal with objects through structural logical processes appears.

8- Increasing objectivity and social raising process leads to moving from egocentrism to thinking of the mutual social relationships.

The following is a summary of Piaget's cognitive development stages:
A summary of Piaget's stages in cognitive development

Stage	Years approximately	Characteristics
1- Sensorimotor	Birth-2 years	The infant distinguishes himself from the rest of the objects. He becomes gradually aware of the relationship between his actions and its results on the environment. Thus, he becomes able to recognize and makes the exciting events last longer. He learns that objects continue to exist even if they were not seen.
2- Preoperational	2-7 years	He uses language. He is able to represent objects through imaginations and words. He is still egocentrist. The world revolves around him. He can't imagine others point of view. He sorts objects according to one dimension and at the end of the period he starts to use the number and develops memorization concepts.
3- Concrete operational	7-12 years	He is able of logical reasoning. He learns memorization concepts in the following order: number (6 years), mass (7 years), and weight (9 years). He sorts objects, and organizes them in series on the basis of dimensions. He understands words of relationship (a is longer than b).
4- Formal operational	12 years and above	He thinks of abstractions and follows logical hypothesis. He gives reasons based on hypotheses. He isolates elements of the problem and treats all the possible solutions regularly. He becomes interested in hypothetical and future matters and ideological problems.

Readiness to learn for (J. Piaget)

It comes to someone's mind a broad question saying: What is the extent of readiness to learn for "Piaget"?

We find the answer to this question at both Dr. Mohyi Eddin Touq and Dr. Abdul Rahman Adas where they think that the developmental readiness to learn for (Piaget) has a relative concept, because limits of learning are subject to cognitive development stage that the child belongs to, and what distinguishes this stage from thinking modes and patterns. Thus, we must not face the child with problems that require actions excelling his cognitive development stage. We also must not disable him of practicing actions of which his cognitive development qualifies him to practice.

In front of this opinion, Dr. Touq and Dr. Adas mention three questions they described as basic questions and worry educators, namely:
- First question: Can we approve Piaget's thoughts about characteristics of each stage, so we rest on them in organizing instructional experiences that suit levels of our children's readiness to learn in different actions.

In this respect (Piaget) says that every child passes by the four stages, in an organized sequence. But ages for each stage are approximate. The child's advancement pace is affected from one stage to another by the formative factors, the environmental and the general cultural factors and what is related to it of personal experience factor. Results of the scientists' studies indicate that there are differences between children from one age in their cognitive development. They may reach in some cases three or four years.

This is from one hand, from the other hand some scientists are tended to say that the child does not think at the same level in all situations. Also, some of the researches that were conducted in England indicate that the development of thinking is done in full gradual progress not in stages each one of them are characterized by special traits. As we see, we can be guided in general by (Piaget's) stages in the gradual development of the child's thinking. However, in addition to that we must seek to understand levels of thinking that our children reached when we organized their learning.

- Second question: If the cognitive development of children is subject to individual differences among them, could the school works to push this development?

Piaget says that the cognitive development is influenced by opportunities of the child's interaction with the environmental stimuli. Thus, providing several opportunities in front of children, to interact and experiment things and to interact and discuss with people, helps a lot to understand their cognitive development. We have already seen together how some schools develop special educational programs to compensate children who join educationally poor environments so as to develop their readiness to learn.

- Third question: Do we comply with the level of cognitive maturity of our children in our organization of their learning? There are two opinions in organizing instructional experiences of children with reference to (Piaget's) thoughts: One of them is demanding the total identification between instructional experiences and the prevailing thinking patterns of the child. The other opinion is demanding the partial identification. The pretext of people of the later opinion is that we must target developing the child's cognitive growth not keeping him where he is. Also, this development necessitates putting the child in situations that require using thinking patterns somewhat higher than his prevailing thinking patterns. Thus, failure of these last patterns in handling the situation leads to tryout the desired most elevated pattern, then to gradually integrate it in his cognitive organization. This later opinion is considered an application for the strategy of organizing learning as for (Piaget) who sees that every child in every age has some things he knows about and has opinions about, but he is not sure of the validity of his knowledge and opinions, especially when he has about them some contradicted or conflicting evidences so that they provoke doubts in his knowledge and opinions.

It is the teacher's responsibility to uncover these matters that are considered a field for the cognitive disequilibrium for the child, which elicit confusion and worry for him. So prepare for him new resources for knowledge that light the path before him for new and successful explanations for these matters. Therefore, he gets rid of the state of cognitive disequilibrium and moves to a state of satisfaction resulting from integration of new experiences in his cognitive organizations.

The teacher must not always wait until states of disequilibrium appear automatically. Instead he has to help him by what he prepares of activities and helps him in performing these activities so he stimulates in him astonishment and questioning.

Application of Piaget's theory in education

On other hand, in the context of the application of Piaget's cognitive theory in education, we find that Piaget's contributions extend to the general educational domain. There are five domains being mentioned by both Dr. Fouad Abu Hatab and Dr. Abdul Majeed Nashawati. They see a potential that Piaget's model to be applied in it. These domains are:

1- It is possible to benefit of such model from the experimental results related to it in the study of behavioral inputs of learners especially from the intellectual cognitive perspective. At the present time efforts are being made to build tests that assess the general school readiness. Getting ready for the different instruction types depends in its core on the cognitive structure that Piaget has reached to.

2- The model benefits in building school curricula, especially with regard to distributing the content of the educational material to different classes. For example, Piaget's results include providing the scientific approach and some subjects related to it in more early age than is common currently. In his opinion it may be at 9-10 years of age.

3- The model helps the teacher in understanding the evolutionary developmental sequences so as to predict for the student when to master subject of learning. He also warns and cautions him of learning mistakes and acquiring difficulties.

4- It can be derived from the model recommendations that are suitable for direct application in situations of intellectual teaching inside the class, including that the student must perform real actions using the materials that consist the learning subject. It is conditioned that the student must do concrete actions by using materials that consist of the subject of leaning. It is also conditioned that actions be significant and direct as much as these materials allow. This requires the analysis of curriculum's content into the processes included in it, then organization of the learning material so that these processes can be made by the learner himself.

5- Piaget's model asserts the importance of social interaction in learning. He thinks that this process liberates the child from being self centered. This indicates the necessity of organizing the collective activity inside the class through the joint projects and discussion sessions and others.

Bruner's Theory of Cognitive Development

J. Bruner was able to develop a theory in cognitive development to the effect that every subject can be taught to children in any age effectively in some of the right intellectual ways. Bruner in his theory studies ways of the individual representing his experiences internally and ways of storing and retrieving representations. He also considers that the issue of theorizing in the cognitive development domain requires paying attention to important points relevant to cognitive development processes. They are the following:

1- The child is willing to separate stimuli from responses during his cognitive development. A great amount of development is occurring when the child is able to do the same response even in case there is any change in the stimulus or the environment surrounding this stimulus.

2- Cognitive development depends on internalization of events through a special memory that is identical with the environment according to an "internal storage" process through which information are stored. This memory is the memory that enables the child to go beyond the information that face him, relying in this on predictions and explanations facilitated by that stored information that was available for him about the world.

3- Cognitive development processes contain increasing abilities to addressing the self and addressing others, symbolically, i.e. through a symbolic linguistic or non linguistic mediator. This seems obvious when talking about the past and future activities and actions.

4- The necessity of finding the organized interaction between the teacher and the learner. With the necessity of taking into consideration the different organized relationships that the culture lost, which affect the relationship of the teacher with the learner. Merely the presence of the child in a certain cultural community, does not mean the fully guarantee his cognitive development, but teachers, family members and other adults must contribute in understanding this culture and delivering it to the child through organized interaction processes.

5- The necessity of using language in cognitive development processes, as a key to this development. Using language facilitates learning and then instruction. Language is the tool that can be used by the learner to give a specific mark to the environment in which he lives.

6- Cognitive growth is characterized by the increasing ability to examine alternates synchronously, i.e. to handle several possibilities in the same time.

Bruner's Stages of Cognitive Development

Bruner's interests were aimed at the representation process that took a basic position in cognitive development for him. His interest in internal representation processes of the external world became evident, in other words in the processes in which the child separates the responses from its controlled stimuli. He develops a system to process information that helps him to store experiences and to retrieve them when necessary.

Bruner reached to identify three stages for representation processes. They are stages or ways used by the human individual in translating his experiences about the world. These stages are:

First: Enactive Representation Stage: This stage is described as the stage of sensorimotor knowledge, where the cognitive development during it occurs through work and action. The child in his every early childhood recognizes events and objects through actions and movements that he is doing towards these events and objects. Action here is the only way through which the child gets to know his environment, and through which he represents his external world. The skills he is performing are sensorimotor skills in particular.

Second: Iconic Representation: It means here representation by using mental images. Cognitive development occurs during this stage through visual visualizations. That is when the child is able to represent the world through visions and spatial images that summarize the action in the time that they are relatively independent from it. The child here remains prisoner of his perceptual world that is basically based on principles of organizing perception such as convergence, resemblance and closing gaps.

Third: Symbolic Representation Stage: Cognitive development in this stage moves along symbols and shapes, during which the external representation is made by language. Considering that language is the most natural specialized system. However, it must be clarified that language is not the one that distinguish between this representation and the previous one, but it seems that using language as a tool for thinking is the important. Since the child resorts to use language as an extension to what he has been doing of indicating objects-that is he refers to objects through the language and gradually the child uses words to replace objects not present now. Therefore, the word for the child is an aspect of the object and this is not a symbolic representation.

The child in this stages becomes able to formulate his experiences in (linguistic and non linguistic) symbols or mathematical and logical equations, which refers to his ability to create ideas and store information that truly represent the external world, and which can be retrieved easily and smoothly.

In short, in Bruner's theory of cognitive growth, we find that he does not believe that there are completely independent stages for cognitive development in spite of the details of the three stages he advocates. The child actually moves from the enactive representation stage to iconic representation stage then to the symbolic representation stage. However, this doesn't absolutely mean that the adult confines himself in his cognitive processes to the symbolic representation only, but means that the symbolic representation becomes more dominant when the child is getting older. Also, individuals represent their experiences practically and iconically throughout all their life span and not in specific age stages of their lives, which relate to the early years of their lives.

Erikson's Theory of Psychological Development

Erikson is considered one of the psychoanalysis school professors who were influenced by Sigmund Freud's theory. However, he was different from the later in terms of his feeling that personality is not determined in early childhood. Instead, its development continues throughout the life span of the human being. In this meaning many felt that Erikson has developed a new model of psychological development that is more comprehensive and humanistic than Freud's model.

Erikson thinks as Freud that there are critical periods of development. He indicates that these periods are characterized by disturbance, or by crucial transformation points, as well as the possibility of going back periods. He attributes that to the radical changes that are happing in the course of the child's development. Also, the growth problem that the child faces in a specific stage of his development, if it wasn't solved then it will happen again in any following stage. However, Erikson was in dispute with Freud in his optimism that failure in a stage would be corrected by success in the following stages. In addition, solving problems in a certain age does not necessarily necessitate a solution for previous other ones.

- Erikson stages of psychosocial development

Erikson's stages of development form a persistent continuous process, consisting of eight stages. The individual, if faced a crisis in any stage of them, must try to overcome this crisis before moving on to the next development stage, if this development was meant to be sound. The following is a brief presentation of Erikson's psychosocial development:

- First Stage: It is a stage that characterized by the child learning to trust or not to trust the environment from birth to eighteenth months. This is the critical period in which the child must develop a sense of self-confidence and in the environment, that feeling that forms the base of the healthy personality of the child. It is the period of overall reliance on others, as the child depends on them in securing his basic needs.

Erikson draws attention to the feeling of trust formation process in the child that it becomes more difficult in the following years, if it wasn't established firmly during the first year of age, because roots of reliance on others lie in it.

- Second Stage: (from eighteenth months to three years). It is a stage characterized by autonomy, or doubt if the child grew up completely dependent on the mother, or who is in her place. The child may learn to successfully control the environment during this period, if he was given the right reinforcements from parents or educators. On other hand, the child who is over protected and taken care of might learn to fear environment. Also, weak care and protection will produce unpleasant experiences, and might produce fears similar to the first case.

The importance of parents, guardians and educators role becomes clear in this stage, in reinforcing the development of the healthy autonomy for the child, by adopting raising styles that secure a kind of balance between tolerance and firmness, so that tolerance wouldn't change to complete negligence, nor would firmness change to absolute domination.

- Third Stage: Initiative vs. guilt (from three to six years). They are the years in which the child develops feelings of sufficiency or inferiority. The child also learns during these years to connect with his peers, how to deal with rules and customs and how to perform school assignments.

The child starts in the stage here of initiative to develop conscience, that is to develop the feeling of right and wrong. Here the important role of parents and teachers becomes clear in developing this feeling. The extreme confirmation of "right" and "wrong" by using severe moral and punishment styles may generate feelings of guilt in the child, which hinder his healthy motives to test himself in wide social world.

- Fourth Stage: Industry vs. inferiority (from six to twelve years).

During this stage the child may head for improving his abilities and skills in terms of facing difficulties, as it appears in the child determination to be able to perform all what he is doing of works.

- Fifth Stage: Identity vs. role confusion (from twelve to eighteen years).

Erikson was known of his interest in development in adolescence. Adolescents are usually busy looking for their identity and their selves. They are either able to achieve their identity or they face what is called disturbance or role confusion and that is because of what happens in their interactions with the world around them.

- Sixth Stage: Intimacy and solidarity vs. isolation (from 18 to 35 years).

In this stage adolescence comes to an end. The individual starts to fill his social role as an adult in his community. So, all the previous development experiences qualify him to practice this role and to participate in intimate and honest relationships with the partner from the other gender. The individual during this stage turns toward a mutual identity reinforced by a suitable marriage, a feeling of intimacy and cordiality is shaped from.

- Seventh Stage: Generativity vs. self absorption or stagnation (from 35 years to retirement).

In this stage a feeling of personal production or (innovation) is generated, which results from generating distinct facts. In spite of having children and engaging in taking care of them, this line in this stage refers to an innovative creative activity for the individual, and reinforces the feeling of production. However, this feeling is not limited to reproduction. Feeling of generativity refers to the individual's style in conveying wisdoms, values and virtues which he gained during his development to the second generation. The only danger that the individual faces here is his long self absorption and his inability to be liberated from the circle of self doubt.

- Eighth Stage: Integrity vs. despair (retirement years):

This stage is the summery of all previous stages. It is on top of it, because its roots lie in early trust, autonomy, active identity and creative production. The individual in this stage finds himself when he contributes in building and creating the new generation, accepts his complete life, realizing that it has a meaning. Therefore, he reaches the stage of integrity and is liberated from the feeling of despair that surrounds some people who faced difficulties in overcoming crisis of their development.

Unit Five

Motivation and Attention

Content:

- Nature of Motivation

- Motivation Concept Development

- Motives Classification

- Individual Differences in Attention and Motivation

- How Do We Increase Motivation in Students?

- Suggestions to Attract Attention of Learners

Motivation and Attention

Nature of Motivation

Before talking about the nature of motivation, we must define each of motive and attention and show the extent of correlation between them.

Definition of Motive:

Motive is the latent energy in the organism that prompts him to act in a certain behavior in the external world. This energy is the one that draws for the organism his goals and ends to achieve the best possible adaptation in his external environment.

Definition of Attention:

Attention is a type of readiness that indicates-in special way- sensory or mental adaptations that contribute in producing perceptual or motor responses or overlap between it. Thus we say about the person who is focusing his eyesight on something that he is ready to see. This situation is a sensory situation and a motor situation at the same time because eyes muscles turn towards the object and focus on it.

Attention-from the standpoint of perception- is a perceptual situation, or say if you wish expectation response and readiness to be influenced.

It becomes clear from these two definitions for both motive and attention-that the later- with its different meanings-nothing but a process of prompting and directing. The human being becomes voluntary aware as well as spontaneously. He also responds according to his interests and attitudes. It is known that kinds of voluntary interest, attitudes and actions fall in the range of prompting and attention. This confirms the fact of the existing relationship between motive and attention.

Thus, motivation concept is used to refer to what prompt the individual to do a specific behavioral activity, and to direct this activity toward a certain direction. Researcher of the people's daily life finds out that behind their behavior several motives. They demand food and look for it when they are prompted by motive of hunger. They seek to demand water and drink when they feel motive of thirst … and so on of motives such as anger, fear, happiness and dignity… etc.

Some of these motives arise from the body's needs related to his organic (physiological) functions such as his need to water, food and sex. Some of these motives arise from the individual's dealing with society such as the need to security, stability, success and appreciation and so on. The first type of motives is called primary or physiological motives, while the second type is called secondary, social or acquired motives.

Before discussing the relationship of motives with the educational process, learning and the role that such motives play in this field, we must identify differences between terms of motives that are being used usually to denote the forces that direct the human behavior towards a specific goal. In this we can look at motives from two basic corners which are:

1- Drives:

They often mean the internal organic stimuli that make the organism ready to produce special responses towards a certain subject in the external environment. Such drives make human behavior enthusiastic. Hunger, thirst and the alike are of innate motives that produce muscular, gland and intellectual responses prompt the individual to fulfill, in addition to the drives that prompt to a suitable adaptation behavior. Compliment, scolding, reward and punishment, and even expecting these matters, are enthusiastic incentives and can not be denied. Then that goals and intentions are strong drives, especially if they had a strong relevance to the individual's needs, and their results are valuable for him.

2- Incentives:

They are the subjects that the organism aims at and direct its responses whether towards or far away from them. Such incentives work to eliminate states of severe emotions such as distress and tension he is feeling. Examples of incentives are food that opposes hunger drive and water that oppose thirst drive… and so on.

It is noticeable that these two aspects of motives-drives and incentives-are not functionally separated. Thirst drive for example prompts the human being to look for water. Water in its turn stimulates thirst drive. We can also notice a kind of overlapping between these two groups of motives in addition to their functional relationship with each other. It is meant here is to show that we can not separate between the two groups of motives (drivers and incentives), instead the relationship between them is existing and they are continuously interacting with such relationship.

The importance of motives from the educational perspective is defined from being an educational aim per se. Stimulating and directing motivation of students and generating certain interests in them, makes them engage in practicing cognitive, motor and emotional activities outside the range of school work. In their future lives such motives are one considered of the important educational aims that any educational system seeks for.

Motivation Concept Development

Talking about the development of motivation concept prompts at first to throw light upon the philosophical points of views that prevailed during past decades and had the direct influence on the look to the human character and on explaining human behaviors.

The issue of motivation nature and theories causes a prolonged debate between psychologists who still until today face difficulties in identifying some other psychological concepts such as intelligence, personality or innovation... etc. Those psychologists created several theories that differ by the difference of their views to human and the human behavior and by the difference of the principles of psychology school to which they belong.

In fact, motivation theories which are currently available especially in educational domain seem of visible usefulness in terms of providing principles and ideas that help the teacher to deeply understand the human behavior, and enable him to create a clear conception about it... This is due to the considerations of the important role that motivation started to play during the few past decades in learning theories and personality theories. Here we will limit the research to four theories or trends that address motivation and tackle most important aspects of motivation, namely:

First: Correlation theory or correlation trend:

This theory was concerned with motivation concepts out of learning theories of behavioral curve or what is called theories of (stimulus-response) from which some important principles can be derived for learning process. Fulfillment states resulting from certain responses, shorthand the need resulting from a behavior, and the proper and direct reinforcement for the desired behavior patterns, are important learning principles and helpful in explaining and stimulating motivation in students.

Second: Humanistic theory or humanistic trend (Maslow's hierarchy) in motivation:

This trend is concerned with explaining motivation and illustrating its concepts related to personality studies. One of most prominent scientists in motivation is Maslow who sees motivation in the human being develops in hierarchy to fulfill needs that he identifies in seven needs organized from the pyramid base to its peak as follows:

1- Psychological needs:

They are determined by very basic types such as food, drink, air, residence. Maslow sees that having food and drink and the fulfilling psychological needs related to them is not the end for human motivation, but this fulfillment leads to liberating the individual from the control of his physiological needs, and to provide the sufficient opportunity for the appearance of a higher level needs.

2- Security and safety needs:

They are needs that represent the individual desires to live in security, peace and tranquility, with the avoidance of worry, disturbance and fear. These needs of security appear in both children and adults by the fast and active movement practiced by the individual in case any emergency appeared threatening safety and security such as natural disasters, wars and epidemics.

3- Love and belonging needs:

They are needs that indicate the individual's desire to create emotional relationships with people in general and with persons and groups important in his life in particular. Such needs result from feelings of the individual's suffering because of the absence of those intimate to him. This is a healthy phenomenon that appears in normal individuals in general. Maslow sees that the individual's contribution in social life is prompted by his need to love, belong and sympathy, and that rebellion and disobedience may result from not fulfilling these needs.

4- Self-esteem needs:

These needs indicate the individual's desire in achieving his distinct self. Fulfilling of this need appears in feelings of trust, efficiency and capability, while not fulfilling it leads to a feeling of inferiority and weakness.

5- Self actualization needs:

These needs indicate the individual's ability in achieving the biggest amount possible of his potentials and abilities. These needs appear clear in vocational and non vocational activities performed by the individual in his adult life, that agree with his desires and interests. Maslow sees that the human being who can achieve his self enjoys a very high psychological health. However, Maslow limits all that to adult individuals only, because children and adolescents won't be able to achieve these needs because of their incomplete maturity and growth. In return, children can be taken care of and their growth can be guided in a way that enable them to recognize their potentials and abilities, and pave the way in front of them to develop and achieve their potentials and abilities in a better way.

6- Knowledge and understanding needs:

These are needs that refer to the continuous desire in understanding and knowledge. They are evident in explanatory activities, in searching for more knowledge, and acquiring the biggest amount possible of information. Maslow sees that knowledge and understanding needs are more evident in some individuals than others. This type of needs plays a vital role in the academic behavior of students, because the process of reinforcing it enables them to acquire knowledge and origins of scientific reasoning, based on internal self motives.

7- Aesthetic needs:

This type of needs denotes the true desire in aesthetic values. These needs are manifested in individuals in their interest in or their preference of arrangement, order, consistency and perfection whether in subjects, situations or activities, as well as in their tendency to avoid repulsive situations where chaos and irregularity prevail. Despite that Maslow admits of the difficulty to understand the nature of aesthetic needs, he believes that the normal individual who enjoys a sound psychological health tends to search for beauty in his nature whether he was a child or an adult and he prefers beauty as an absolute value that is independent from any material utility.

The following is a figure illustrates Maslow's hierarchy of motivation needs.

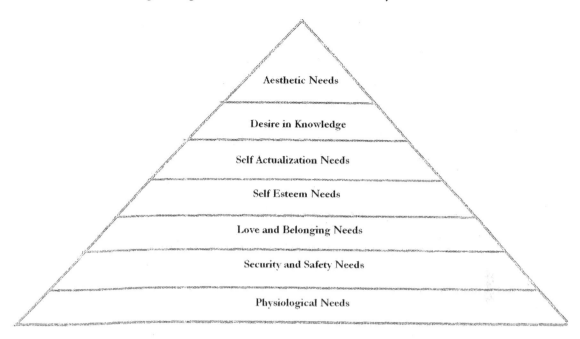

It is noticeable that most of these needs presented by Maslow were built on philosophical ideas that acknowledge the innovative ability of the human being. Also these needs are free from the experimental character in its scientific meaning, where their results were derived by clinical and non clinical observations and interviews, so it is difficult to judge the validity of these results. However, this does not mean the uselessness of such theory, and its benefit in education and social raising domain, because the parents, teachers and educators realization of the fact of the hierarchy of human motives, and the necessity to fulfill some of the lower motives in order to be able to fulfill motives in the higher level, enlightens these people on several matters that must be observed in the process of raising and educating children.

Third: Cognitive theory or cognitive trend in motivation (Weiner) and (Atkinson):

Cognitive explanations of motives assume that the human is an intelligent creature, and enjoys a will by which he can take conscious decisions the way he likes. Explanations also assume the existence of basic needs for people and seeking to understand the nature of environment and its components.

These explanations also confirm concepts that are more related to central averages such as expectation, purpose and intention, because the intellectual activity of the individual provides him with a personal motivation inherent in him and refers to behavioral activity as an end in itself not as a mean.

According to this trend, people work hard because they enjoy working and because they seek more understanding (controlling the obscure and the unknown). Motivation in the cognitive trend is based on plans, interests and decisions, and considering what leads to success or failure. Therefore, expectations of success and failure play an important role in the conceptual analysis of motivation.

- Bernard Weiner and attribution theory in motivation:

This theory was recently circulated in the framework of studies in terms of handling the individual's motivation toward success, resisting failure, and handling the individual's attributions for his success and failure reasons whether in academic achievement or other which is caused by motivation effect in the individual's reactions.

The famous and contemporary American scientist (Bernard Weiner) in the University of UCLA developed this theory and published it in an image of a distinguished widespread and applied theory. This theory was used in explaining reactions of the normal and abnormal individuals in different fields. Weiner called this theory (Theory of pleasure and pain). He sees in one of his studies that pleasure and pain are achieved by the individual after achieving understanding which is considered the basic stimulus for the individual's action and movement.

Weiner says that the need to the concept is the one that leads students to wonder about circumstances of success or failure they are facing in school learning. This scientist sees that students and individuals in their different positions attempt to explain why what happened is happening, or why it happened in the way it happened, so as to attribute such circumstances or refer them to specific reasons. Therefore, students may attempt to explain their relationships and grades by listing many factors such as effort, ability, mood, luck, help, interests and clarity of instructions.

Weiner refers causes that students attribute to their success or failure to three main groups:

First: related to internal causes (factors in the person himself) with external causes such as ability, mood, and effort. External causes include task difficulty, the teacher's trends, luck and help from others.

Second: stable or unstable causes, such as stable ability and unstable mood.

Third: controllable or uncontrollable causes. You can control the amount of help you get but you can't control luck or the mood in the exam day.

All the reasons by which the individual explains what happening for him of outcomes can be classified in the previous dimensions.

Weiner sees that these dimensions are all important in the individual's motivation, his internal orientation and his external orientation in attribution of the individual for his success or failure reasons. Weiner gives examples about the relation of feeling or shame. If the individual's attribution for his success was to external factors, this leads him to be grateful. While if attribution of failure was to external factors, it may be followed by a feeling of anger.

As for the third dimension, it appears to have a relationship with expectations about the future. For example, if students attributed their success or failure to stable factors such as ability or test difficulty, they expect that they are going to fail or succeed in similar tasks in the future. However, if they attributed outcomes to unstable factors such as mood and luck, he expects attributions and reasons to change in the future if he faced the same tasks.

Whereas the control dimension in the individual is associated with feelings of satisfaction and future expectations if he attributed success to controllable factors, student may feel proud and that he can achieve that success in the following tasks in the future. However, if he attributed success to uncontrollable factors, the student feels grateful and hopes that luck will continue in making him succeed in the future although it is uncontrollable and cannot be repeated.

(Atkinson-1965) and motivation:

Atkinson formulated a theory of motivation of broad lines in respect of relation with achievement motivation and instructional tasks. He explained at first that tendency to achieve success is an acquired motivational readiness, meaning it is something learned. It consists in respect of its connection with behavioral activities a function for three variables or factors that identify the students' ability to achievement and they are:

1- Motive to reach and achieve success

This motive indicates the individual proceeding to perform a task with additional enthusiasm and activity, in order to acquire the experience of possible success. However, this motive has a natural outcome that becomes evident in another motive, which is avoiding failure. The individual attempts to avoid certain important opinions in fear of failure that he might face in performing such opinions. Success achievement motive lies behind students' difference in their achievement levels, where the students' achievement level (or their achievement motivation) rises with the rise of this motive, and vice versa.

2- Possibility of success

Possibilities of success in any task are high, moderate or low possibilities. Easy tasks do not provide the individual with an opportunity to pass through a success experience whatever was the motive degree to achieve success he has. Whereas in the very difficult tasks, individuals with their different motive degree to achieve success do not see they have ability to perform such tasks, while in the cases of moderate tasks, the evident differences in the motive degree to achieve success affect performance in a clear way and different with the difference of motive.

3- Value of success incentive

The more the task is difficult, the more that required to increase the value of success incentive. The more the task is difficult, the more the incentive (reward) must be bigger to maintain a high real level. Difficult tasks related to low value incentives do not stimulate the individual's enthusiasm in order to perform these tasks with high motivation. The individual himself is the one who estimates the difficulty of the task and its incentives.

At the end, Atkinson sees that when the individual is performing a certain task he is facing a challenge of the kind of courage and refrainment, where his motive prompts him to achieve success over courage, at the time that failure avoidance motive prompts him over refrainment and withdrawal.

With respect to application in the classroom, the above three changes may become strong or weaken through instructional practices. It is important that the teacher works to strengthen success possibilities and weaken failure possibilities, and work to strengthen success achievement motive in his students, through passing by success experiences, and presenting tasks with a reasonable degree of challenge and soluble.

Fourth: Psychoanalysis theory or analytical trend

This Freudian theory is different from the methods of correlational, humanistic and cognitive theories, whether in terms of concepts or in respect of its following imaginations of the human being, his behaviors and the development of his personality. It uses the concept of suppression, instinct and unconsciousness when explaining behavior.

According to this theory there is a kind of interaction between early childhood experiences and the unconscious desires resulting from the drives of sex and aggression, where fathers and parents prevent children from the free expression identified by these two drives, which drive these children to suppress this behavior and deposit in the unconsciousness... However, these suppression processes do not end the effectiveness of sex and aggression drives, but they exercise their effect in identifying behavior from inside unconsciousness itself, where expressing suppressed motives and desires comes in indirect behavioral forms, which sometimes materialize in practicing some patterns of negative behavior directed towards the self or the society.

In short, the scrutinizer of what is presented by psychoanalysis theory of explanations and concepts for the development of human behavior, helps the teacher to understand more of the students behavior, and enables him to achieve interaction with them in a way that move instruction process to what is better.

Motives Classification

There are two types of motives. Motives that arise from the body needs related to his organic physiological functions such as the need for food, water, sex and to avoid cold, heat and pain. This type of motives is not learned or acquired by the individual but it exists in him innately. If he learned something he pertains to it. It is to control it. For example, when the student postpones the fulfillment of hunger motive until the study ends and goes home, directing it to a special direction, or responding to incentives without responding to other related to it, like what happens when the individual responds to a certain kind of food and not responding to other kinds… and so on.

There are motives or needs come as a result of the individual's growth, his communications with others, facing the general life circumstances, and what these circumstances necessitate such as the need to social appreciation and to success and feeling security… and so on.

The first type of motives is usually called primary or biological motives and the second type is called secondary or psychological motives.

However, dividing motives into primary and secondary may be a tricky process sometimes, as though the reader thinks that the primary motives are more important than the secondary motives. Therefore, he prefers instead to use the term biological motives that include that motives to which we don't know an evident biological basics such as hunger, thirst, sex and motherhood. He also prefers the term psychological motives to refer to these motives to which we don't know evident biological basics such as possession, respect, excellence, control and so on.

Primary or biological motives:

These motives are identified by heredity and species of the organism. They are directly related to his life and his basic biological needs such as hunger motive, thirst motive, sex motive, motherhood and fatherhood motives and other motives we have referred to.

The primary motives are almost the motives that affect the behavior of the organisms without the human being. Effects of these motives appear clearly in his behavior and acts. Thus, it is easy to control behavior of such organisms according to controlling the biological motives that control these organisms.

Secondary or psychological motives:

They are the motives that arise as a result of the individual's interaction with his environment and the different social circumstances he lives in. These motives play a tangible role in the individual's life that surpasses in most cases the role played by the biological motives that can be described as being easy to meet somehow. The child's need for food (that is a primary biological need) is fulfilled by the mother through nursing or by giving him meals wherever he is hungry, but soon he'll grow up and starts crying to draw his mother's attention and before long he'll develop new motives that he learns through interacting with others especially the parents. In this respect we find the American psychologist Abraham Maslow develops a hierarchy of human motives that includes the basic needs for such motives (They were mentioned in detail at the beginning of this unit).

Individual Differences in Attention and Motivation

All members of mankind are similar among them in bodily and intellectual qualities and emotional, social and ethical traits. They are subject to general laws in perception, learning and emotions, including attention and motivation... However, they are also different among them in these qualities and traits. For example, the students in one class you find differences evident among them in academic achievement, in the way of facing problems of the daily life, and in moods of interaction, in addition to their being different in tendencies, orientations and values.

Attention laws, that is the readiness that creates responses, have a role in identifying the level and the extent of motivation force towards performance. This explains the nature of the individual's differences between people... This means in whole that attention has an effective role in identifying levels of individual differences from one hand and in the difference of motivation levels in individuals.

In an explanation of that we find students who enjoy high motives for achievement, they are hard workers and persistent in their works. They follow their future plans. The reason behind that is originally due to the high degrees of attention and readiness in this category which supports the motive effectiveness toward achievement in a sound way. Unlike that category of students who have low achievement motives.

In the context of individual differences and the extent to which they are affected by motives, studies revealed that differences in the individual's behavior who have high achievement motives and those who are prompted by the motive of avoiding failure, since members from the first category attempt examining competitive problems and issues with a moderate difficulty and achievement, while individuals from the second category tend to choose very easy problems or very difficult and illogical.

All that require increasing the need to know the different differences between members, in order to be directed to different activity styles academically, professionally and socially that fit their willingness and interests from one hand, and the demands and needs of the society from other hand, and that is in the framework of working to activate perceptual attention situations towards responses to motivation and stimulation.

Discovering the individual differences between individuals in their different growth stages led educators to adapt concepts of readiness and motivation to different instruction stages levels so as to fit that difference. Also, knowing the individual differences helped in developing training programs for different careers that fit these differences, also there were different drives that also fit with such differences.

How Do We Increase Motivation in Students?

Looking for increasing motivation in students leads to review concepts related to learning motive, which is exemplified in willingness to do good work and to succeed in that work.

Motivation to learning refers to inner state to the learner that leads him to pay attention to the instructional situation and to engage it with directed activity, and to continue in that activity until learning is achieved. Stimulation alone does not produce learning and does not increase its motivation. However, we can say that learning doesn't happen without stimulation and activity. Therefore, the concept of motivation to learning and increasing it in students must include the following elements:

a. To do an activity directed to these elements.

b. To continue and maintain the activity for a sufficient period of time.

c. To pay attention to some of the important elements in the instructional situation.

d. To achieve learning goal.

On other hand, the recent researches indicated that the human being likes curiosity by his nature. These researches provide us with a new starting point to direct learning towards the independence of this need from one hand and to achieve more motivation for students towards learning from the other hand. The human being is seeking new experiences. Also, he is enjoying a new learning, and feels satisfied when he solves a problem or develops tasks through organizing the behavior of curiosity that forms a basic foundation for learning, innovation and psychological health, since one of the main tasks in learning is how to foster curiosity, and using it to achieve learning and increase motivation towards it.

It can be said that students who have the basic motive to achievement, motivation degree in them to learning is in its highest levels, when success chance is moderate. Perhaps the first step of learning is to provoke confusion about what is familiar, even the basic source of stimulation for the motive in the classroom is the teacher himself. We can also say that the student's interest in the educational material is affected basically by the teacher's enthusiasm degree to it.

To foster the motive of curiosity or the motive of achievement is one of the most important issues in the process of achievement and instructional development for the learner. Also, one of the matters that achieve the increase in the instructional motive is the necessity to provide instructional atmosphere full of freedom and security in the school and class environment, through accepting and fostering the students' ideas and not by resorting to physical punishment in class. In addition, we must provide the opportunity of success in front of all students in some of the materials and tasks. This is done by taking into consideration the students willingness to learn in planning instructional activities, and by presenting the students achievements by referring to what they can do.

Suggestions to Attract Attention of Learners

There are some orientations which are like suggestions that contribute in stimulating and reinforcing learners' motivation, which supports learning efficiency for the learner and enables the teacher to use activities and events to achieve this. The following is the most important of these suggestions arranged and detailed as mentioned by Dr. Yousef Qattami in his book "Psychology of Learning and Class Learning":

- To place the student in situations of research and exploration, because curiosity is basic for learning and innovation. The teacher's role is identified by fostering research and developing exploration in his students.

- To use questions style instead of providing information.

- To use recent and new concepts in the learning of students.

- To use discovery.

- To decrease chances of supervision because supervision creates boredom and lessens the attention of the students.

- To link motivation with achievement and its outcomes.

- To use doubt style in what the learner knows because it increases his motivation to learning.

- To provide an instructional atmosphere full with love, security and freedom.

- To lessen chances of sarcasm and mockery in the student's opinions.

- To avoid using physical punishment and link it to class learning.

- To provide opportunities of success because success leads to success.

- To provide class materialistic environmental circumstances facilitating learning, such as using and verifying sensory stimuli.

- To use styles of positive reinforcement to elevate learning.

- To avoid typical practices in the procedures of class learning.

- To develop real goals can be learned by the learner.

- To identify the learner of what he achieves of success no matter what the degrees of this success were.

- To provide opportunities in from of students to express what they have acquired of experiences and to use them in solving instructional problems.

- To use styles of encouraging because this positively affects the learner, especially the successive learning, it increases the continuity of the learner's performance and lessens chances of his inhibition and its negativities.

- To increase chances of cooperation that is considered effective for students who are prompted by the motive of avoiding failure and to increase chances of competition in students who are prompted by the achievement motive.

References

1- Ausubel, David Paul, Educational Psychology, a cognitive View, N.Y Holt Rinehart and winston, 1968.

2- Bichler, R.F., Psychology Applied to Teaching. Boston, Houghton Mifflin Co. 1978.

3- Blair, Jones and Simpson, Educational Psychology (2nd ed) The Mcmillan Company N.Y 1962.

4- Bruner, Jerome, S., and others, Astudy of thinking, Wiley, 1956.

5- Bruner, Jerome, s., 1974, 1977.

6- Crow, Lester Donald, Educational Psychology, Rev. ed. N.Y American book 1963.

7- Foss, B.M New Horizones in Psychology. Britain 1967.

8- Gage, N.L. and Berliner, D.C, Educational Psychology, Rand McNally Education Series Colege Publishers Co. chicago, 1981.

9- Gange, R., Conditions of Learning, (2nd ed) N.Y Holt Rinehart and winston Inc 1970.

10- Galloway, C. Psychology of learning and Teaching. Mc Graw Hill Book co. N.Y 1976.

11- Gates, A. Educational Psychology. The Mcmillan Co. N.Y 1942.

12- Gibson Janice, T. Educational Psychology. New Century, Educational Division, Meredith corporation, N.Y 1968.

13- Guilford, J.P General Psychology, Van Norstand, N.Y 1939.

14- Lewin, K, Field theory of learning, N.S P.E. No 41. Year book.

15- Mursell, J. L Psychology of Secondary school Teaching (Revised edition). N. Y

16- Rush and Zimbardo, Psychology and lift (8thed) Scott, Forsman and Company, Glen View, Illinois 1971.

17- Sandstram, C. I., The Psychology of childhood and adolence, Methuen, London. 1966.

18- Sartain, Norh Strange and chapman.

19- Thorndike, E.L Educational Psychology. 1903.

20- Travers, John. F Educational Psychology N.Y Harper & Row 1979.

21- Turner, J Psychology of thinking MC Graw Hill, 1952.

22- Wood worth r.s Experimental Psychology, Hemry Holt & Co. New ed 1972.

23- Wright, Taylor, Davis, stuckin, lee and Reason, Introducing Psychology. Penguin books. Middlesex, England 1970.

Principles of Modern Education Psychology

This book is presented to teachers, educational psychologists and every seeker of knowledge, hoping this will be a step in the march of scientific research and follow up the fact of the position of modern educational psychology in a world in which researches of this human science have developed and reached to cognitive facts that science connoisseurs including teachers, learners and educational researchers to both follow and be familiar with them.

Auther: Dr. MARWAN ABUHEWAIJ. PH.D., in Education .Assistant Professor, Arabic Language teaching, Defence Language Institute Foreign Language Center. Presidio of Monterey, CA 93944.

Specialization: Foreign Language education and language acquisition, Teaching, Counseling, Research in High Education Teaching, Higher Education Lecture, Curriculum development , training and evaluation.

Publications:
= Measurement and evaluation in Education.
= Behavior, Social, Educational and health Sciences.
= Introduction to Educational Psychology